THE ROYAL PREROGATIVE
1603-1649

𝕿𝖍𝖊 𝕽𝖔𝖞𝖆𝖑
PREROGATIVE
1603-1649

A Study in English Political and
Constitutional Ideas *by* FRANCIS D.
WORMUTH, *formerly Sterling Fellow
at Yale University, Instructor in Government at Indiana University*

KENNIKAT PRESS
Port Washington, N. Y./London

TO MARY

PREFACE

THE political controversies during the reigns of the first two Stuarts centered on one question—the nature and extent of the royal prerogative. This study began as an examination of ideas on the prerogative in that period, but it soon became clear that in no case could the prerogative be treated by itself; always it was part of a larger system of ideas. In the final result the prerogative has come to occupy no very considerable place, and for that reason the title of this monograph may appear misleading. But no more representative title suggested itself, and the title is perhaps apt in that it intimates the point of view from which the different arguments and classes of arguments are considered.

A more serious defect is that of arrangement. The treatment is in a sense circular; different sectors of opinion are examined as they impinge upon the central problem. It is obvious that no sustained chronological description was possible, and this is a grave shortcoming. Even more deplorable is the fact that under this method of treatment topics which might well be examined independently have been wrenched apart and distributed in fragments in the various chapters. Only the hope that this method may have merits as well as defects has emboldened the author to publish the study. The examination of seventeenth century thought from this point of view has led him to certain novel conclusions about royalist theories, political and legal, which he hopes may prove acceptable to others. And in particular he is anxious that Roger Manwaring be relieved at last of the censure of the House of Lords, and recognized as a theorist at least of the stature of Maistre, if he may not come in the first rank of champions of sovereignty.

Acknowledgement is due to the Sterling Fellowship Fund of Yale University for the assistance which made possible the completion of the study. The author owes a great personal debt to those

Preface

who have been his teachers, advisers, and critics: to Professors Frederick G. Marcham, Carl Becker, George H. Sabine, and George J. Thompson of Cornell University, and Professors Wallace Notestein and Francis W. Coker of Yale University. Dr. Goldwin Smith of the University of Iowa supplied copies of all the manuscript sources cited, and a wealth of other material which contributed to the conclusions herein stated. Finally, the author has derived from a whole generation of graduate students at Cornell and at Yale not only assistance and instruction, but the inestimable satisfaction of comradely adventuring in scholarship.

FRANCIS D. WORMUTH

Indiana University
November, 1938

TABLE OF CONTENTS

CHAPTER I

CHAPTER II

CHAPTER III

CHAPTER IV

CHAPTER V

CHAPTER VI

CHAPTER VII

THE ROYAL PREROGATIVE
1603-1649

THE NATURE OF THE STATE

I. *Law as the basis of society; command as the basis of society; the distinction between king and state.*

II. *Government and adjudication; the sanctity of property; the issue of taxation.*

I

THE Whig view of the constitutional controversies in England before the Civil War, the treatment popularized by Macaulay and Gardiner, reduces the issue to a simple opposition of absolutism and popular right, with Parliament in the double rôle of champion of the people's right to participate in government and defender of the legal rights of subjects against illegal oppression by the monarch. The more recent interpretation takes account of the fact that both the representation in and the ambitions of Parliament were far from democratic, and therefore emphasizes the second function the Whigs attributed to Parliament in these disputes, defense of the time-honored common law of England against the new philosophy of law as the will of the king. This point of view assumes that Parliament rather than the court was in the right in specific disputes as to the power of the king at common law, a contention which Parliament itself was unable to prove conclusively and which was disputed with considerable success by the court lawyers. But it would be profitless to inquire which party had the better precedents, for the issues which arose in the seventeenth century were in the main novel and could be settled by no appeal to earlier practice. Of more interest and importance than actual historical precedent are the opinions of the different controversialists as to what the laws of England truly were, the generalized systems or philosophies for the support of which appeal was made to history.

The current interpretation of these disputes supplies guidance here. The Parliamentary faction did indeed regard the laws of England as judges today regard the common law; they considered them a body of rules rooted in past practice and in the reason of judicial decision, rather than mere legislative enactments. The royalist party on the other hand tended to take the position that law was voluntaristic in character; it derived its binding force not from any inner merit but from the will of a sovereign. But the issue is not the simple issue between Aquinas and Austin. To begin with, there were more than two schools of thought; and none of these schools can be adequately described in terms either of pre-existent law or of law as will. The royalist party contained not only philosophers who builded upon a theory of sovereignty—a not entirely Austinian theory of sovereignty—but lawyers who rooted royal power in the law of England. The Parliamentary party always professed allegiance to a scheme of static law, but the actual claims of the Long Parliament fell little short of sovereign authority, and the common law rights of subjects were made to stoop to legislative fiat. The doctrine of royal sovereignty matured in the early part of the century was confronted by a doctrine of Parliamentary sovereignty.

But this resolution of the controversy was the work of the Civil War. At the beginning of the seventeenth century the direction of the argument was not clearly perceived, and indeed the earlier positions, at least on the part of the Parliamentarians, had not been unequivocally accepted. Specific disputes arose, and particular positions were taken; only in the 1620's did Parliament generalize its ideas into a philosophy of pre-existent law; and only in the '40's did this yield to the claim of trusteeship by Parliament which was in fact sovereign power.

These disputes were conducted primarily in terms of national law. Political theories might be employed as well, and particularly by the royalists such theories were introduced; these were not intended to supersede national law but to explain it. It was assumed that a proper understanding of monarchy would supply the solution of the problems of constitutional law. And such an assumption underlay the Parliamentary position also, and now and again found expression in writings and speeches, though only Hooker reduced the Parliamentary philosophy to a coherent system.

Generally speaking, two rival approaches were employed in discussing monarchy in terms of political theory. Superficially these conflicting conceptions might appear to occupy common ground, for writers of both schools paid lip-service to Aristotle's analysis of governments into monarchies, aristocracies, and democracies. But in fact the two points of view rested on radically different assumptions, and had nothing in common. One method of treatment, which might be called the jural or jurisprudential, assumed that national government, whatever its form, derived its authority from national law, and that the various forms were merely the kinds of mechanism which national law might direct. This approach is Aristotelian indeed in its acceptance of variety in government; but it is quite un-Aristotelian in the attention it gives to the jural sanction of government, and in its treatment of governments as artificial or derivative. Those who employed the jural method did not necessarily espouse the Parliamentary cause in the series of disputes which led to civil war. Men who thought in terms of national law alone were likely to do so. Hooker, who best supplies a jurisprudential basis for the Parliamentary party, very firmly set the law above the king. But men whose minds were formed on Bodin and the Roman lawyers were likely to apply to the royal power not merely the tests of local law but the law of princes. They thought in terms of sovereignty. There were certain critical powers of government which, if vested in a single person, necessarily implied complete sovereignty; and the further characteristics of the monarchy were elaborated by a political science which had no relation to national law. This school was much more friendly to the prerogative than the English common lawyers, yet it proceeded on the same assumption, that monarchy was a creature of law.

Opposed to the legalistic conception of monarchy was a school of thought which might be called naturalistic; this school was necessarily royalist. Whereas the legalists treated law as primary and monarchy as secondary and derivative, the naturalist school regarded monarchy as a natural institution, and law as a derivative from monarchy. The kingship was the standard of reference by which national law was measured. These writers were Aristotelian in that they considered government a natural thing, producing rather than resulting from law; but they so emphasized the naturalness of kingship that it is hard to see how they could admit of any other form of government, possessing a merely jural origin and exercising a derivative authority.[1]

The legalist and naturalist philosophies of kingship were also rival philosophies of society. The point of view which Hooker represents is somewhat medieval. Organization, superiority and subordination exist in society, as indeed they exist in the universe, by virtue of the informing presence of law; law and order are the fundamental facts of society. As Sir John Eliot construed Livy,[2] "that tearme of multitude cannot passe into the name & title of the people, to consolidate that body, but by the ciment and coagulation of the Lawe, the operation of that spirit that works congruitie in all things. This brings opposites together, & the greatest dis-

---

[1] Bacon as Chancellor told Parliament in 1621: "First concerning Monarchy. Schools may dispute but tyme hath tried. States under other formes are either not apt to spreade or, if they ripen or grow greate, are apt to dissolve." "Pym Diary," *Commons Debates, 1621* (ed. Notestein, Relf, and Simpson) iv, 8. In his *Argument in the Case of the Post-Nati* he said that monarchy was the only natural form of government; others were creatures of law. *Works* (ed. Spedding) xv, 198.

[2] *The Monarchie of Man* (ed. Grosart) ii, 42.

tances to meet contraries & extremities. This easily reconciles, metall with metall, element with element, fire with water, heaven with earth: the Sunne by this has his glorie in the day, & that faithful witnes, hir beautie, in the night; all the lesser starrs & planets in their spheares have their particular light & motions from this power, & with the rest that generall harmonie & consent in the obedience of the greater." The royalists, on the other hand, were concerned to demonstrate that kingship was the organizing principle in society, as command was the organizing principle through the universe: the king, like the parent or master in his family, and like God among the angels, was the significant feature which informed the whole of society with order. The relation of superiority and subjection, and the institution of command, were the facts from which law and organization derived. Without a sovereign, said Edward Forsett, "no people can ever as subjects raunge themselves into the order, and communitie of humane societie, howsoever, as men, or rather as wild savages, they may perhaps breath a while upon the earth." [3] James defended the bishops in similar terms. "Heaven is governed by order, and all the good Angels there; nay, Hell itself could not subsist without some order; and the very devils are divided into legions, and have their chiefetaines: how can any society then upon earth, subsist without order and degrees?" [4] According to Bacon there are three "platforms or patterns which are found in nature of monarchies": [5]

the first is that of a father, or chief of a family, who governing over his wife by prerogative of sex, over his children by prerogative of age, and because he is author unto them of being, and over his servants by prerogative of virtue and providence (for he that is able of body, and improvident of mind, is *natura servus*) is the very model of a king. . . . The second is that of a shepherd and his flock, which Xenophon saith, Cyrus had ever in his

[3] *A Comparative Discourse of the Bodies Natural and Politique* (London, 1606). For further quotations from Forsett see p. 69 ff., *infra.*
[4] *A Premonition*, in *Political Works of James I* (ed. McIlwain) p. 126.
[5] *Argument in the Case of the Post-Nati*, in *Works*, xv, 197-8.

mouth. . . . The third platform is the government of God himself over the world, whereof lawful monarchies are a shadow.

The function of the king was sometimes identified with that of the soul or of the sun: he was the mainspring of society.

> Now the soul is *toto in toto, & tota in qualibet parte,* whole in the whole body, and whole in every part of it: Even so the King inanimates and informes the whole collective body of the people, and every particular man of it, of what degree, quality, or profession soever. . . .
>
> Againe, as the King is the soule, so also is he the Sun of the Commonwealth, according to the Psalmist, *His Throne shall be as the Sun.* The Sun is *Sponsus naturae,* the beauty and Bridegroom of Nature, appointed by God to rule the Day, and it runs from one end of the Heavens to the other, so that nothing is hid from the heate and light of it, but every creature from the Cedar to the Shrub receives benigne and propitious influences from it: so a King (as before I told you) is *Decus Israelis,* the beauty of Israel, the supreme Magistrate, the effects and influences of whose government, as peace, justice and religion extend over the whole Kingdome . . . so that high and low, rich and poore, one with another, and all together owe their *bene esse* unto him.[6]

The legalist school, therefore, or at any rate that portion of it which became identified with the Parliamentary party, felt that the king derived his authority from the laws, and was, as Coke expressed it, but a "hieroglyphic of the laws." [7] The supporters of the Stuarts urged that the laws derived their authority from the king; they were, as Bacon said, "the great organ by which the sovereign power doth move." [8] To use a theological analogy, the Parliamentary theory was close to the deistic idea of a universe governed by law; the royalist theory was like the doctrine of divine immanence.

The Parliamentary view of society, though not advanced with directness and cogency equal to that with which a number of royalist writers presented their views, was certainly more in

---

[6] Henry Valentine, *God Save the King* (London, 1639).
[7] Calvin's Case, 7 Reports 11b.
[8] *Op. cit.,* p. 200.

harmony with the temperament of the times. Perhaps indeed it was this very fact that made the royalists assume the offensive. The supremacy of law was a familiar heritage from the middle ages. Law and the institutions which had their being in law were enduring, objective; they formed the sustaining medium in which human affairs were conducted. The most nearly opposite idea of law was that of Hobbes and Filmer. To these men law was voluntaristic: it sustained nothing, but was sustained by the will of the sovereign. Filmer thought it a crushing objection to the legislative power of the Parliament to ask what became of law when the Parliament was dissolved: once the sovereign whose continuous will was necessary to maintain law disappeared, there could be no law. The usual royalist argument did not go so far as Filmer; it did not treat regal power as mere arbitrary will. Command was the nature of government, but command was a relation rather than a fiat. The king possessed a natural authority, like the shepherd of the flock or the paterfamilias, and it had a purpose and function which colored its character. Legislation was not an act of will; it was an act of protection and guidance. Still, in the royalist scheme law necessarily rested upon the will of a man—that was precisely the force which sustained it—and analytically therefore it could be declared to be imperative. All royalist theorists specifically declared that a despotic and iniquitous law was still law.

Hobbes and the royalists agreed also that without a sovereign there could be no organization, actual or legal, among the men who by virtue of kingship constituted a society; they were a "headlesse multitude." [9] But here too there is a fundamental disagreement. Hobbes made the king the essence of the commonwealth, but he was an abstracted essence; he was the genuine representative of the people, because the multitude had conferred upon him their power. To the royalists the king exercised not a derivative but a natural authority. Society was drawn into co-

---

[9] *Trew Law of Free Monarchies*, in *Political Works of James I*, p. 68.

herence by authority emanating from the king; the state existed, but it was as a projection of the king.

The Parliamentarians, relying upon an analogy of objective dominating law rather than dominating persons, contradicted both Hobbes and the orthodox royalists. The political organization of the commonwealth, in which the king occupied a chief office, was quite different from the personal relation between the king and his subjects. Allegiance and law were two different things: in the first sphere, the subjects were dependent upon the king as a natural person; in the second, king and subjects both occupied pre-appointed places in a system defined by a law external to both.[10] It followed that the Parliamentarians repudiated the royalist identification of king and state, and asserted that there was a clear distinction between the two.

The point had been repeatedly urged on the continent by those writers who found it expedient to set up the nation against the prince. Mariana in his *De Rege et Regis Institutione* contended for the separate existence of the nation, which enabled it to remain headless and to deliberate about the choice of a ruler. Hotman and his friends made the same argument. And royalists insisted that the distinction was treasonable and spurious.

In England the question was raised now and again. Thomas Scott wrote of *The Puritan*:[11]

> He'll not a traitor be unto the King,
> Nor to the Laws (for that 's another thing
> Men dream not of, who think they no way can
> Be traitors unto many, for one man). . . .

And Eliot charged against Buckingham, in his speech of impeachment: "Have not your lordships heard him also ever mixing and confusing the king and State, not leaving a distinction between

---

[10] See p. 21, *infra*.

[11] *The Interpreter* (1622), reprinted in Firth, *Stuart Tracts, An English Garner*, p. 233.

them?"[12] An anonymous correspondent of Charles I reversed the charge. In enumerating the types of seditious persons that vilified the Duke of Buckingham, he listed "Innovators, *Plebicolae,* and King-haters. At the latter end of Queen *Elizabeth,* it was a phrase to speak, yea for to pray for the Queen and State. This word *State,* was learned by our neighbour-hood and commerce with the Low-Countreys, as if we were, or affected to be governed by States. This the Queen saw and hated. And the old Earl of Oxford his Proposi-tions at her death, they awakened King James to prevent this humour, and to oppose the conditions and limitations presented unto him by the Parliament."[13]

The first overt appearance of the controversy was the trial of Strafford. Strafford was impeached for treason against the nation; he was impeached for attempting to subvert the fundamental laws of the kingdom, and Charles' intervention could not save him. The point was erected not merely into political theory but into law: "I have heard lawyers say that in the case of Lord Strafford's treason when he was convict by Bill of Attainder as against the state, then the treason being found against the kingdome, and the will being shown of it [it] resided in the King and Kingdome jointly to pardon him."[14] It was as a representative of a coordinate power that the Parliament went to war with the King, and later brought him to trial for high crimes and misdemeanors.

But at this point we should recognize that a significant change has come into Parliamentary theory. In the view of Hooker, which

---

[12] Forster, *Sir John Eliot,* i, 550. The reports of the speech in the Lords Journal and in Rushworth lack this passage, but for once Forster appears reliable. "8 lines pinned upon the Court gates, May 1627" repeat the accusation:

        Rex and *lex* are of a sounde,
        But *Dux* doth *rex* and *grex* confounde.

Historical Manuscripts Commission, *Twelfth Report,* Part IX (1891) p. 547.

[13] *Bibliotheca Regia* (1659) p. 290. This is the opinion which Judge Jenkins also con-troverts, in his *Lex Terrae:* "We maintain that there is no State within this kingdom but the King's Majesty, and that to adhere to any other State within this Kingdom is High Treason." *Judge Jenkins* (ed. W. H. Terry) p. 47.

[14] Sloane Mss., 1457.

can properly stand as the pure type of jural theory, only the law defined the competence of king and subject, and only the law could vindicate itself in case of transgression. This is hardly a creed for a revolutionary party. The French monarchomachs in the sixteenth century had encountered this difficulty, and they had evaded it by substituting for the notion of a basic law the theory of an original contract. The king was bound by compact to his kingdom, and thus it became plausible that the kingdom by its officers vindicate its rights against the king. Here was an instrument apt for rebellion, and as such it was used by Huguenots and Jesuits indifferently.

The Long Parliament accomplished a similar result without explicit use of the contract theory. Parliament represented the kingdom, it was charged with a trust by the kingdom; the king also was a trustee, and if he failed in his duty the fundamental laws required Parliament to perform it for him. The fundamental laws thus led to the law of sovereignty, rather than the sovereignty of law. Most of the Parliamentary apologists candidly professed the contract theory, but it did not receive official confirmation by Parliament until the Rump House of Commons, unable to justify the regicide and the abolition of the House of Lords in terms of law, made the appeal to political theory. [15]

II

The Parliamentarians were able to exchange a *Rechtsstaat* for a *Volksstaat* without unsettling completely their belief in a static society and objective right. They were obliged to adopt a view of government which was political rather than legal, dynamic rather than static, in order to compete with the dynamic theory of kingship set forth by the royalists. But this sacrifice of congenial notions was made for the sake of a deeper permanency, a fixed order which, in their minds, underlay government itself. They believed in the

---

[15] Gough, *The Social Contract,* p. 94.

primacy of property, and to them one of the chief functions of government was the protection of property.

It would be a mistake to give this notion the clearness which it later took in John Locke's mind. The Parliamentarians were, at least theoretically, conservatives in all respects, and they did not inquire as to which of the established customs they venerated was historically or logically prior. But the bias of their thought is observable in their treatment of government. Sir John Eliot, in his *Monarchie of Man,* recognizes two functions of monarchy, government and adjudication. Adjudication was the preservation of property rights, of *meum* and *tuum.*[16] Royalist writers, discriminating between state policies which looked abroad into the field of international affairs and questions of local administration, denominated the former "matter of state" and the latter *"meum* and *tuum."* For the royalists the second field yielded to the necessities of the first; for the Parliamentarians, the first field must yield to the second.

Frequently quoted was that adage of Seneca's which Professor McIlwain has said epitomizes the political philosophy of the middle ages: "To princes belongs government; to private persons, property."[17] England was perhaps the last stronghold of that medieval doctrine; by the end of the sixteenth century absolutism and the Roman law had made Loisel's phrase a fact if not a moral truth on the continent: *Qui veut le roi, si veut la loi.* Nor were the English unaware of their singularity. For them, private property was guaranteed by Magna Carta, and was safeguarded by the Parliamentary control of taxation. And it would be wrong to regard Parliamentary taxation as an exercise of governmental power over

---

[16] To Sir Edward Coke, it seems, jurisprudence consisted only of property law, criminal law, and judicial power. In the *Prooemium* to his *Fourth Institute* he describes the plan of the *Institutes:* "In the two former parts of the *Institutes* we have principally treated *De communibus placitis,* and of those two great Pronouns (*Meum* & *Tuum*). In the Third we have handled *Placita Coronae,* and Criminall causes. But because *Rerum ordo confunditur, si unicuique jurisdictio non servetur,* We in this Fourth and last part of the Institutes are to speak of the Jurisdiction of the Courts of Justice within this Realm."

[17] *Growth of Political Thought in the West,* p. 394.

a subject people. Parliament was not an authority which imposed taxes. It was a representative body, and was thought to be, in more than a figurative sense, the nation itself; and when it voted subsidies to the king it made a free gift on behalf of the people, rather than levied taxes on the people. So Parliament in its taxing function was nothing more than an institutional crystallization of the sanctity of property, an evidence of, rather than an exception to, the complete immunity of property from governmental control.

Parliament as the protector of property rights was particularly prominent in men's minds, and had been since the time of Fortescue, who argued that because the French commons had acquiesced in the king's usurpation of the taxing power,

The French kyngs have yearly sythen, sett such chargs upon them, and so augmented the same chargis, as the same Commons be so impoverished and distroyyd, that they may unneth [scarcely] lyve. Thay drynke Water, they eat Apples, with Bred right brown made of Rye. Thay eate no Flesche, but if it be selden [rarely], a littil Larde, or of the Entrails, or Heds of Bests sclayne for the Nobles, and Merchaunts of the Lond. They weryn no Wollyn, but if it be a pore Cote under their uttermost Garment, made of grete Canvas, and cal it a Frok. Their Hosyn be of like Canvas, and passen not their Knee; wherfor they be gartrid and their Thyghs bare. Their Wyfs and Children gone bare fote; they may in non otherwise lyve. [18]

Onslow, the Speaker of the House of Commons in 1566, boasted that "by our common law, although there be for the Prince provided many Princely Prerogatives and Royalties: yet it is not such, as the Prince can take money, or other things or do as he will at his own pleasure without order; but quietly to suffer his subjects to enjoy their own, without wrongful oppression, wherein other Princes by their liberty do take as pleaseth them." [19]

The Tudors might differ with the Parliament over some point of prerogative revenue, but in the main they fully admitted the Parliamentary control of taxation. It was the Stuart period that

---

[18] *Absolute and Limited Monarchy* (ed. Fortescue-Aland, 1714) p. 17.
[19] *Hansard's Parliamentary History*, i, 719.

brought innovation. The increasing expense of government, coupled with the improvidence of the Stuarts, made the question of revenue an urgent one. The attempt of the Commons to "deal merchant-like" in supplying the king made the court take a higher strain than ever, made them exalt the prerogative and employ it in the collection of new impositions. As a sort of prelude to the Stuart reigns we find Serjeant Heale arguing in the Commons in 1601, on feudal principles, that all property ultimately belonged to the Queen.[20] The House laughed him down, and "Mr. Mountague of the Middle Temple" replied to Heale that "there were no such precedents." But the decision in Bate's Case, upholding the power of the king to levy import duties at will,[21] seemed to create such a precedent, and a great alarm went abroad as to its consequences. The Commons protested to James in 1610, "we profess, touching that Judgment, that we neither do, nor will, take upon us to reverse it; but our Desire is, to know the Reasons, whereupon the same was grounded; and the rather, for that a general Conceit is had, that the Reasons of that Judgment may be extended much farther, even to the utter Ruin of the ancient Liberty of this Kingdom, and of your Subjects' Right of Propriety of their Lands and Goods."[22]

Generally speaking, the assaults upon property during the Stuart period took two forms, legal and philosophico-theological; and both of these arguments made their appearance early in the reign of James. In 1610 the Bishop of Chichester preached at Whitehall that "Goods and money were Caesar's; and therefore they were not to be denied unto him"; the Commons were seriously disturbed. James apologized for the Bishop, assuring his Parliament that "If I had bene in his place, I would have added two words, which would have cleared all: For after I had told as a Divine, what was

[20] D'Ewes, *Journals of All the Parliaments During the Reign of Queen Elizabeth* (1682) p. 633.
[21] See *infra*, pp. 54, 72.
[22] *Commons Journal*, i, 431.

due by the Subjects to their Kings in general, I would then have concluded as an Englishman, shewing this people, That as in generall all Subjects were bound to relieve their King; So to exhort them, that as we lived in a setled state of a Kingdome which was governed by his owne fundamentall Lawes and Orders, that according thereunto, they were now (being assembled for this purpose in Parliament) to consider how to help such a king as now they had; and that according to the ancient forme, and order established in this Kingdome."[23] But James' conduct toward his Parliaments only increased the uneasy fear of the gentlemen of England that *meum* and *tuum,* with its safeguard, the Parliament, was imperilled. Sir Robert Phelips in the Parliament of 1625 made a melancholy speech, reminding his hearers that England was the only nation in which the Three Estates still retained the taxing power. The preachings of Sibthorpe and Manwaring raised this apprehension to a higher pitch. Archbishop Abbot, because he believed that "there is a *Meum* and *Tuum* in Christian commonwealths, and *according to Laws and Customs, Princes may dispose of it:* That saying being true, *Ad reges, potestas omnium pertinet, ad singulos proprietas,"* refused to license Sibthorpe's *Apostolic Obedience,* and was forbidden to perform his ecclesiastical functions in consequence.[24] The temper of the time is shown by the advice with which "a learned gentleman of the Inner Temple" persuaded Worrall, chaplain of the Bishop of London, to revoke his allowance of Sibthorpe's book: "What have you done? You have allowed a strange book yonder! Which, if it be true, there is no *Meum* or *Tuum*! no man in England hath anything of his own! If ever the tide turns, and matters be called to a reckoning; you will be hanged for publishing such a book!"[25]

The most alarming expression of all was the advice which Sir

---

[23] *Political Works,* p. 308.
[24] *Archbishop Abbot's Narrative of his Sequestration from all his Ecclesiastical Offices,* in Firth, *Stuart Tracts, An English Garner,* p. 327.
[25] *Ibid.,* p. 329.

Dudley Carleton gave on behalf of the King to the Commons in 1626 when they expressed resentment at the imprisonment of Digges and Eliot. "I beseech you, gentlemen, move not his majesty with trenching upon his prerogatives, lest you bring him out of love with parliaments. In his messages he hath told you, that if there were not correspondency between him and you, he should be enforced to use *new counsels*. Now I pray you to consider what those new counsels are, and may be. I fear to declare those that I conceive. In all Christian kingdoms you know that parliaments were in use anciently, until the monarchs began to know their own strength; and seeing the turbulent spirit of their parliaments; at length they, little by little, began to stand upon their prerogatives, and at last overthrew the parliaments throughout Christendom, except here only with us. And indeed you would count it a great misery, if you knew the subjects in foreign countries as well as myself; to see them look not like our nation, with store of flesh on their backs, but like so many ghosts and not men, being nothing but skin and bones with some thin cover to their nakedness, and wearing only wooden shoes on their feet; so that they cannot eat meat, or wear good clothes, but they must pay and be taxed unto the king for it. This is a misery beyond expression, and that which yet we are free from!" [26] The threat of "new counsels," and the repeated reference by Sir John Coke and other court spokesmen to "new ways" of taxation increased the uneasiness of the Commons. Charles himself in the same year gave some occasion for apprehension. He told the two Houses: "Remember that parliaments are altogether in my power for their calling, sitting, and dissolution; and therefore, as I find the fruits of them to be good or evil, they are to continue or not to be." [27] A royal proclamation following the dissolution of Parliament in 1629 announced that there would be no further Parliaments until the people had "come

---

[26] Forster, *Sir John Eliot,* i, 555.
[27] Forster, *op. cit.,* i, 527.

to a better understanding of Us themselves."[28] Heylyn may be taken to express royalist opinion when he says that the summoning of the Short Parliament was unseasonable, "in regard that Parliaments had been so long discontinued, and the people lived so happily without them, that very few took thought who should see the next."

Undoubtedly concern over property was only one of the factors that set the temper of the Long Parliament. More prominent was the religious issue; more prominent also, in all probability, was the ambition of the country gentry to attain a position in political life commensurate with their economic importance. Nor is it likely that the fear of confiscation of property by the crown had any very solid foundation. Both the legal advisers of Charles and the clerics who preached divine right disavowed any intention of confiscating property, and there is no reason for doubting their good faith. The doctrine of the Ship-Money Case was limited to emergencies; and the Canons of 1640, in which Laud expressed the philosophy of divine right, scrupulously reserved property to the subjects. But the Parliamentarians were not satisfied with anything less than complete immunity of property. St. John protested against ship-money:[29]

I⸱ is not that Shipmoney hath been levied upon us, but its that right whereby Shipmoney is claymed, which if it be true, is such, as that it makes the payment of Shipmoney the gift and earnest penny of all we have. . . . Ship-money by these opinions is not due by any peculiarity, in Ship-money: but Ship-money is therefore due, because his Majesty is the sole Judge of the danger of the Kingdome, and when, and how the same is to be prevented, because his Majesty for the defence of the Kingdome, may at his will and pleasure charge the people, this is the ground. . . . by these opinions there is a surrender made of all Legall defence of propriety, that which hath bin preached, is now judged, that there is no *meum* and *tuum* between the King and the people. . . .

---

[28] Steele, *Catalogue of Tudor and Stuart Proclamations,* i, 186.
[29] *St. John's Speech to the Lords Concerning Ship-Money* (London, 1641).

Nathaniel Fiennes as savagely attacked the Canons:[30]

If Kings were of *Divine Right*, as the Office of a Pastor in the Church, or founded in the prime Laws of Nature, as the power of a Father in a Family; then it would certainly follow, that they should receive the fashion and manner of their government, onely from the Prescript of Gods Word, or the Lawes of Nature, and consequently, if there bee no Text, neither of the *Old* nor *New Testament,* nor yet of any Law of Nature, that Kings may not make Lawes without *Parliaments,* they may make Lawes without *Parliaments,* and if neither in the Scripture, nor in the Law of Nature, Kings be forbidden to lay taxes or any kind of impositions upon their people without consent in Parliament, they may do it out of Parliament: and that this was their meaning, they expresse it after in plaine termes, for they say that Subsidies and taxes, and all manner of ayds are due unto Kings by the Law of God, and of Nature.

These arguments may have arisen out of a serious concern at the royalist denial of the complete sanctity of property, or they may have been merely intended to embarrass the crown at a vulnerable point. But they reveal a basic preconception of the Parliamentary party. Behind society, beyond the reach of political power as such, was property right.

---

[30] *Speeches and Passages of this Great and Happy Parliament* (London, 1641) p. 50.

Chapter II

THE ORIGIN OF GOVERNMENT

I. *The patriarchal theory; the rule of Calvin's Case; the royalist argument from history.*

II. *Conquest; prescription; compact; the primacy of law.*

I

A POLITICAL theory ordinarily provides some historical origin of government, or ascribes its force to some constitutive act. Theorists of the seventeenth century built very heavily on arguments of historical and jural origin. And despite the wide difference of opinion on the nature and justification of authority, all agreed on the historical source of political authority. Raleigh, Coke, Bacon, Filmer, Dugdale—a hundred writers on topics historical, political and legal might be cited to show the unanimity of opinion.[1] The father had originally exercised paternal authority over his family. As the family grew to a clan and then an association of clans, his authority passed into the royal. By conquest his dominion was extended over other peoples, and they came into the same relationship to the ruler his children had occupied. The king possessed over his subjects the despotic power which the Mosaic law and Roman law recognized in the father over his children and his slaves.

---

[1] The introduction to the Commons Journal of James I recites: "Order, the Lustre of Nature, guided by a first Essence, put all Government into Form: First, in two, who, by Procreation according to the Rule of Power (increase and multiply) made a Family, with one Head; by Propagation, a Tribe, or Kindred, with one Elder, or Chief; by Multiplication, a Society, a Province, a Country, a Kingdom, with One or more Guides or Leaders, of Spirit, aptest, or, of choice, fittest, to govern.

"This Division, sorting itself into Proprieties, fell, in Parts of Right, greater or smaller, to some Tribe, Kindred, or elective Change of Person. *Vicissitudo rerum,* the Herald of Time, doth warrant this to be the true Original Pedigree of Government."

This explanation, naturally, gave comfort to those who regarded political authority as a domination or command of the ruler over his subjects, and considered law a dynamic force by which the king held society in order. It might be employed casually, as Cecil employed it in defending Elizabeth's prerogative in the debate about monopolies: "I am sure there were Law-makers before there were Laws." [2] Or it might be worked into a formal justification of royal authority by writers like James and Filmer; with these men, it supplied the other half of the argument for the royalist attitude toward government described in the preceding chapter. Philosophically, command was the nature of government; historically, also, that had been its character.

The royalist implications of this view of history can be found even in so unfriendly a writer as Coke. In his opinion in Calvin's Case [3] Coke argued that between king and subject was a personal relation of superiority and subjection, deriving from the pre-legal status of the kingship.

By this law of nature is the faith, ligeance, and obedience of the subject due to his sovereign or superior. . . . This law of nature, which indeed is the eternal law of the Creator, infused into the heart of the creature at the time of his creation, was 2,000 years before any laws written, and before any judicial or municipal laws. And certain it is that before judicial or municipal laws were made, kings did decide causes according to natural equity, and were not tied to any rule or formality of law, but did 'dare jura'. . . . Now the reason wherefore laws were made and published, appeareth in Fortescue, . . . and in Tully, lib. 2, Officiorum: 'at cum jus aequabile ab uno viro homines non consequerentur, inventi sunt leges.' Now it appeareth by demonstrative reason, that ligeance, faith, and obedience of the subject to the sovereign, was long before any municipal or judicial laws. 1. For that government and subjection were long before any municipal or judicial laws. 2. For that it had been vain to have prescribed laws to any, but to such as owed obedience, faith, and ligeance before, in respect whereof they were bound to obey and observe them: 'frustra enim feruntur leges nisi subditis et obedientibus.'

---

[2] D'Ewes, *Journals of All the Parliaments During the Reign of Queen Elizabeth* (1682) p. 649.
[3] *Howell's State Trials*, ii. 629. See *infra*, p. 50.

This was good royalist theory, to which Coke rather incautiously committed the common lawyers. But it by no means went so far as the royalist arguments. Coke admitted an extra-legal and personal relation between king and subject, but this extended only to the question of allegiance. It determined the status of the post-nati; it explained the king's authority over denization; it buttressed the laws against treason. But all the questions which came in issue between king and subjects in Coke's time were left to the arbitrament of law, for the king had two capacities, one personal and one public. In the latter rôle his relations with his subjects were purely legal, and the subjects' obligations to him were to that legal entity, that corporation sole, the crown, rather than to the person of the king. The king in his natural capacity possessed no political authority; that was attached to the office. Questions of property and of personal right were governed by the law.

The royalists on the other hand refused to accept this distinction between the natural capacity and the political capacity of the king. The royalists conceived of the king as a natural man, who possessed a large natural authority as paterfamilias, but had consented to exercise it by law within the limits of the legal office. Concerning his obligation to obey the law there was some difference of opinion. Bacon evidently thought that except for the prerogative the pre-legal power of the king had been quite taken away.[4] James seems to have admitted that his actions could violate law, but to have insisted that he possessed some sort of extra-legal competence to do so—his theories will be discussed later. Sir John Hayward, however, pressed the historical argument to its furthest extremes. Since the king was the original source of law he could modify it at pleasure. Brief extracts from his *Right of Succession Asserted*[5] will show the course of his argument.

---

[4] See his *Brief Discourse upon the Commission of Bridewell,* in *Works* (ed. Spedding) xv.

[5] The quotations are from the edition of 1683. The work was originally published in 1603 under the title, *An Answer to the First Part of a Certain Conference concerning Succession, published not long since under the name of R. Dolman.*

What helps now do you imagine, that the people have assigned to their Prince?

The first, you affirm to be the direction of Laws. But it is evident, that in the first herbical Ages, the people were not governed by any positive Law, but their Kings did both Judge and Command, by their word, by their will, by their absolute power; and, as Pomponius saith, *Omnia manu a regibus gubernabantur:* Kings governed all things, without either restraint or direction, but only of the Law of Nature.

. . . For Kings in ancient times did give judgment in person, not of any formality in Law, but only according to natural equity. . . .

But because it grew both troublesome and tedious, for all the People to receive their Right from one man; Laws were invented, as Cicero saith, and Officers also appointed to execute the same.

Another Original of Laws was thus occasioned: when any People were subdued by Arms, Laws were laid like Logs upon their necks, to keep them in more sure subjection. . . .

The second help, which you affirm that Commonwealths have assigned to their Kings, is by Parliaments and Privy Councils. But Parliaments in all places have been erected by Kings. . . .

First I will preface, that no Prince is soveraign, who acknowledgeth himself either subject or accountable to any but to God. . . . In regard of this immediate subjection, Princes are most especially obliged to the Laws of God and of Nature: for Baldus, Alexander, Speculator, all Interpreters, the Law itself, do affirm, that Princes are more strictly bound to these Laws, than any of their subjects. . . . If therefore a Prince doth profess that he will bear himself regardful of the accomplishment of these Laws, he doth not condition or restrain himself but maketh an honourable promise of endeavour to discharge his Duty, being tyed thereby to no scanter scope than he was before. . . .

Again, when the Promise is not annexed to the Authority, but voluntarily and freely made by the Prince, his Estate is not thereby made conditional. . . . And therefore by all Laws, both of Conscience and State, the Prince is bound to perform his Promise; because (as the Master of Sentences saith) God himself will stand obliged to his word: yet is not the authority, but the Person of the Prince hereby affected; the person is both tyed and touched in honour, the authority ceaseth not, if performances do fail.

The whole force of this argument rests on the proposition that a sovereign cannot bind himself. Originally kings possessed absolute authority, and any laws which they might make they could terminate. This authority they passed on to their descendants with the right to the crown. Philip Hunton,[6] who was perhaps the ablest of the Parliamentary pamphleteers during the Civil War, agreed that this was true of absolute monarchies, but insisted that England was by the original contract a limited monarchy. But both of these writers approached the subject from the viewpoint of general political theory. The common lawyers concerned themselves neither with Hayward's claim of absolutism nor with Hunton's rebuttal. To them the English kingship was not primary, and the source of law; law was primary, and 'the source of the kingship. The king by the law of England had succeeded to the throne; the law of England also invested him with certain affirmative powers. Those powers were by no means unlimited; their bounds were marked out by the laws which conferred them.

II

It has been suggested that Coke in Calvin's Case made a needless concession to a school of thought which in general he opposed. A later Whig controversialist with more acuteness insisted that government took its rise in voluntary institution. "There is no other original of magistracy to be learned from sacred or profane history; for though the patriarchs had the government of their own families, (which, by reason of their long age, were very numerous) yet that right was derived from the law of nature, and not from any civil obligation."[7] But if Coke conceded the extralegal obligation of allegiance, the royalists on their side were ready to admit the necessity of the institutive act upon which this writer insisted. Of all the theorists of the time, only Sir Robert Filmer refused to admit that between a patriarchal monarchy and a lawful monarchy a great gap existed. The one was a sociological fact: it was an operating political unit. The other was a *de jure* rule: it had a legal as well as a natural existence.

---

[6] *Treatise of Monarchy*, 1643. The theoretical part of this work was republished in 1689 and is to be found in *Harleian Miscellany*, vi.

[7] *Essay upon the Original and Design of Magistracy* (c. 1689), *Harleian Miscellany* i, 4.

The royalist writers ascribed the jural origin of the state to "submission." Bacon listed four sorts of submission: there was submission to patriarchal rule, submission from admiration of virtue, submission to a military leader through gratitude—or, we take it, fear—and submission to a conqueror.[8] But although submission was required to make the king a lawful governor, it did not, as we have seen, mean the rule of law in the kingdom. For a time the king governed by his own will, according to natural equity; eventually, for his own convenience, he promulgated laws.

Apparently the force of the submission rested on the oath of the conquered—for conquest was the usual occasion for the establishment of a jural rule. Some writers, however, felt that the passage of time was required, to give a prescriptive right to the conqueror or usurper. Samuel Daniel in his *Civil Wars* thought that sixty years of uninterrupted Lancastrian rule cut off the Yorkist right; the judges

> . . . though they knew his claim was fair, in sight,
> Yet thought it now lacked the fair face of right,
> Since for the space of three score years the crown
> Had been in act possessed, in three descents . . .
> That Wrong, by order, may grow right by this,
> Since Right th' observer but of Order is.

That there were vague notions of the acquisition of right by conquest, even by conquest of one's own land by an enemy, is evidenced by Cowley's *Oliver Cromwell*. In a dream-dialogue which the poet held with the devil, the tempter urged him to admit the lawfulness of the Protector's rule, because it was established by conquest. Cowley replied that Cromwell's was not a genuine conquest, since it arose by insurrection from within the land, and not by invasion from without. The fact that Cowley felt obliged to brand Cromwell's rule a usurpation seems to show that he was constrained to admit conquest a legitimate source of authority.

---

[8] *Argument in the Case of the Post-Nati, Works,* xv, 199-200.

But ordinarily no distinction was made between usurpation and conquest. Bishop Overall in the Convocation Book of 1606 stated that a Christian owed the duty of obedience to any *de facto* government; here apparently there is not even a requirement of "submission." And in general the tendency was to regard the present settlement as right, and not to inquire too closely into its origin. The advice of Francis Osborne was unrepresentative only in being cynical: "*Submit* quietly *to Any Power* Providence shall please to mount into the Saddle of Sovereignty, without enquiring into their Right *for Conscience sake.* . . . He that suffers his *conscience* to mislead him in civil Obedience, makes his Guide a stumbling-block; not considering that All Governments now extant had their foundations laid in the dirt, though time may have dried it up by Oblivion, or flattering Historians licked it off." [9]

With the exception of Hobbes the royalist writers were reluctant to admit of any other jural origin of government than submission, which was merely a euphemism for conquest. But it was ordinarily said that government might lawfully derive from divine institution, compact, and conquest. [10] The only cases of divine institution were in the Old Testament; existing governments took their rise in human action. Those theorists whom we have called jurisprudential in contrast with the naturalism of the extreme royalists most willingly discussed compact. The contract theory was an obvious one, and moreover was one with which men were familiar through the Latin authors. They credited the historicity of the inevitable passage in the *Institutes* and said very seriously of the Romans that "by a law which is termed Regia, that is to say Royal, the people have derived into the emperor their whole power for making laws." [11] Those theorists who were thoroughly under the

---

[9] *Advice to a Son,* in *Works* (1682) pp. 60-62. Compare *Leicester's Commonwealth* (1584-ed. 1904) p. 155: "from the beginning of the world unto this day, either among Gentile, Jews, or Christian People, you shall find that the sword hath been alwayes better than halfe the title to get, establish, or maintaine a Kingdome."

[10] See, for example, Hooker, *Laws of Ecclesiastical Polity,* Book VIII, Chap. ii, 5.

[11] *Ibid.,* Book VIII, Chap. vi, 11.

influence of the Roman law believed that the political contract necessarily vested complete power in the king: *Sed et quod principi placuit, legis habet vigorem, cum lege regia, quae de imperio eius lata est, populus ei et in eum omne suum imperium et potestatem concessit.*

The theorists who did not take their jurisprudence from the Roman law saw no necessity of absolutism. The contract prescribed certain powers in the king, certain rights in the subject. The compact included not only the original terms, "which for the most part are either clean worn out of knowledge, or else known unto very few, but whatsoever hath been after in free and voluntary manner condescended unto, whether by express consent, whereof positive laws are witnesses, or else by silent allowance famously notified by custom reaching beyond the memory of man. By which means of after-agreement, it cometh many times to pass in kingdoms, that they whose ancient predecessors were by violence and force made subject, do grow even by little and little into that most sweet form of kingly government which philosophers define to be 'regency willingly sustained and endured, with chiefty of power in the greatest things.' " [12]

Hooker and the others who spoke of a contract in the early years of the seventeenth century used it merely as a device for initiating the state. Like Burke's contract, it was permanently settled and irrevocable; it was merely a peg upon which the laws of the kingdom could be hung. It no more needed to be a historical fact than Rousseau's social contract. To men who felt, like Hooker and Rousseau, that no settlement could be just which was not voluntarily instituted, it meant merely that in proper states this test of justice had somehow been complied with. For Hooker a single original consent by the society is necessary, not a continuing individual consent as with Rousseau: "to be commanded we do consent, when that society whereof we are part hath at any time

---

[12] *Ibid., loc. cit.*

before consented, without revoking the same after by the like universal agreement. Wherefore as any man's deed past is good as long as himself continueth; so the act of a public society of men done five hundred years sithence standeth as theirs who presently are of the same societies, because corporations are immortal; we were then alive in our predecessors, and they in their successors do live still." [13] Obviously this will not stand a very searching criticism; equally, it was not intended to. Hooker places authority in law rather than contract; the contract is merely a rationalization of the law.

The common lawyers did not feel it necessary to make this rationalization. They contented themselves with asserting the legality of the law. The king's dominion antedated law, and this made it necessary to admit a personal relationship of superiority and subjection between king and subject. But the legality of government could be no older than the law itself. The powers of king and Parliament were alike defined by the common law, which antedated the Roman conquest and was indeed of inconceivable antiquity. The assumed and unformulated justification of the rule of law was probably this. The common law contained a principle the operation of which sanctified its jurisdiction, the principle of prescription. By prescription the common law had entrenched itself forever in Britain. Coke might bewail the fact that the Parliament rolls and statutes of the 'ancient Britons' had been lost,[14] but he had better cause for rejoicing, for the discovery of the prime establishment of the common law would have dissolved its magic prescriptive right: "for if there be any sufficient proofs of record or writing to the contrary, albeit it exceed the memory, or proper knowledge of any man living, yet it is within the memory of

---

[13] *Ibid.*, Book I, Chap. x, 8.

[14] "Some fragments of the Statutes in the raigns of the abovesaid [Saxon] Kings do yet remain, but not only many of the Statutes, and Acts of Parliament, but also the Books and Treatises of the Common Laws both in these and other Kings times, and specially in the times of the ancient Brittons (an inestimable loss) are not to be found." *Second Institute, Proeme.*

man." [15] In the absence of evidence that once it had not prevailed in England, the common law was justified, and self-justifying: its formula might be said to be that which the king sometimes employed, *teste meipso.*

This implies, of course, that law has an objective existence, and is not mere will. When the Parliamentarians in 1640 transformed their *Rechtsstaat* into a *Volksstaat,* they abandoned this assumption. The royalists, to whom law was merely the command of the king, always espoused a voluntaristic theory of law.

---

[15] *Coke on Littleton,* 115a.

CHAPTER III

THE POLITICKS

I. *The fundamental laws; sovereignty; the limits of sovereignty; the right of rebellion; equity and justice.*

II. *Government and God; the theory of divine right; the theory of divine power.*

I

ON A lower level of thought and argument than these high debates as to the source and justification of political authority stood a body of discussion of what we would call today political science—called in that day "the politicks." There were in this field many principles upon which men of all parties agreed. Such agreement resulted in part from the fact that this was a distinct body of thought, which at many points, at least, did not touch the larger issues upon which men differed; it was the case also that the implications of political science for political theory were not always perceived. It is true as well that there were many men who were not interested in controversy on the higher level of political theory, and they contributed to the notion that a single set of agreed principles of government was obtainable. This body of thought deserves distinct treatment, for at many points it supplemented, at many points contradicted the more general philosophies of politics.

Stock discussions of "the politicks" usually began with Aristotle's types of government, and the vices and virtues of monarchy, aristocracy, and democracy. The royalists, at least, found monarchy more appropriate than any other form of government. "There be precedents and platforms of monarchies, both in nature, and above nature, even from the monarch of heaven and earth to the king, if you will, in a hive of bees. And therefore other states are creatures of law; and this state only subsisteth by nature."[1] But this meant only that monarchy was a better sort of government than the other two; it did not mean that it was more lawful. A lawful monarchy was strictly analogous to a lawful democracy.

At the opening of the seventeenth century political discussion acquired further philosophical apparatus. Greek thought was supplemented by French thought. Not only was it true that any government must fall into one or another of the Aristotelian categories; it was also true that every government differed from every other in respect to its native constitution, its "fundamental laws." Every nation, by virtue of its individuality, had a peculiar history, a peculiar population, peculiar customs from which arose these fundamental laws. The fundamental laws were justified, not by their logicality and universality, but precisely by reason of their local character; they were justified because they came from a particular milieu and were adapted to it. What the fundamental laws of France actually were depended upon the purpose of the expositor; they usually included the Salic law of succession, and they might embrace the principle of the inalienability of the royal demesne, the right of the Three Estates or of the Parlement of Paris to participate in government, the orthodoxy of the king, or any of a number of such propositions.

The English as well as the French were aware of national custom; and like the French they considered it a native growth peculiarly adapted to native conditions. This was, of course, merely an affirmation of the validity of national laws and national customs, cast in a form acceptable to a generation tutored in the medieval notion that an appropriate and unique law existed for each of the grades, orders, and localities into which human and divine affairs were distributed. If it did not win belief on the ground of truth, it

---

[1] Bacon, *Argument in the Case of the Post-Nati, Works* (ed. Spedding) xv, 197-8.

might at least claim allegiance on the ground of utility. The sceptical no doubt held the opinion later expressed by Pascal:[2] "Upon what shall man found the economy of the world which he wishes to govern? Shall it be upon the caprice of each individual? What confusion! Shall it be upon justice? He is ignorant of it. Certainly, if he had known it he would not have established this maxim— the most general of all that are current among men: that each should follow the customs of his own country. . . . A meridian determines truth; after a few years of possession fundamental laws change; right has its epochs. . . . Montaigne is wrong; custom should be followed only because it is custom and not because it is reasonable or just."

The idea of fundamental laws was already old in France when the English appropriated it. The controversies of the sixteenth century between Ligueurs and Huguenots, absolutists and monarchomachs, had been cast in terms of national law; on one level, at least, they had been simply disagreements over the true constitution of the French monarchy. This distinction between the fundamental laws and customary private law was the more easily drawn because the two systems to some extent conflicted; the Salic law of succession to the throne was inconsistent with the private law of inheritance. The ideas of the English had not been so explicitly formulated as those of the French, because they had behind them no such career of constitutional controversy as had the French. And the distinction of emphasis, the selection from among common laws which the employment of the term fundamental laws implies, was unknown to them, because with the English there was no inconsistency between the ordinary private law of the realm and the fundamental laws. The term does not appear in English writing until the end of Elizabeth's reign, and it seems clear that the English first met it in the French controversialists they read so avidly at the time. It did not receive formal discussion in polemical

---

[2] *Pensées*, VII.

works until the Civil War;[3] in the reign of James it was used rather casually. It was a welcome expression, for it gave Englishmen a jurisprudential basis for their political habits, by bringing them into analogy with the different practices of foreign lands; it enabled them to speak of English ideas and English institutions in the terms of political morphology. In this useful capacity the expression passed into several statutes.

The fundamental laws were not identical with what today we call principles of constitutional law. They included such principles, as Sir Thomas Crew, Speaker of the House of Commons in 1625, informed Charles I: "Your Majesty's imperiall diadem shines the brighter in that it is inamel'd and compast with a beautiful border of the antient and fundamentall lawes of this kingdome, which as synewes, hould the bodie of the Common wealth together, & are suitable to the nature of the people, & safest for the Sovereign."[4] But what we should call rules of private law were also included among the fundamental laws. The Commons in proposing the Great Contract in 1610 assured the King that feudal tenures were not "imperiall" by the civil law, nor were they "ligament of government" by the common law, but in the opinion of Sir Julius Caesar "this contract will make a stronge and deepe alteracion in the fundamentall lawes of theis estate, which is a great mischief, and trencheth further then maie be forsene in tyme, or endured when it cometh."[5] Tenures might well be fundamental laws, though they were not "ligament of government"; they might be

---

[3] A tract of 1643, entitled *Touching the Fundamental Laws,* discusses the subject in detail.

[4] Eliot, *Negotium Posterorum* (ed. Grosart), i, 50.

[5] *Parliamentary Debates in 1610* (Camden Society, ed. Gardiner) p. 178. In *The Great Question Resolved. Whether a King of England Can Make Wars and Alliances Without Notifying it before to his Two Houses of Parliament* (1673), published in Thomas Brown's *Miscellanea Aulica* (1702), it is said (p. 274): "there was a design in the beginning of King James' Reign to take away tenures, by a Statute expressly made to that purpose, but it was resolved by the Judges, that such a Statute had been void, because the Tenures were for the defence of the King and Kingdom. . . . Nay, many Acts made against the King's Prerogative have been nulled and repealed by Parliament itself." Hutton in his opinion in Hampden's Case referred to the same resolution of the judges on tenures, and approved the doctrine. But see the opinion of the judges in 1610, *Lords Journal,* ii, 581.

so deeply rooted in time, so well suited to the "policy" of the nation as to be fundamental. The fundamental laws were not so much laws as experience, not so much commands as precepts. The early seventeenth century was cautious, backward-looking; with Coke, it turned to question *"pristinam generationem"*; it revered precedents. The ancient laws were fundamental, and reliable, because of their antiquity.

Each of the fundamental laws carried the sanction of time and experience; each was independently and internally valuable. Only rarely, as in the case of feudal tenures, was a rule of law submitted to external evaluation and *a priori* criticism by an inquiry as to whether it was a rule of public law. The distinction between public law and private law was dimly understood,[6] but it was not utilized, because it did not tell what the seventeenth century considered important about a law; it was a formal, a mechanical method of criticism which did not deal with the worth of a law.

The character of the fundamental laws thus unsuited them for an exact definition of government. Instead, theorists concerned with the properties of the state drew upon the more precise formulations of the civil law. The usual definition of sovereignty was derived from that source. A sovereign community was of right independent of all foreign control. Internally, "the state or soveraignty consisteth in 5 points. 1. Making and annulling of laws. 2. Creating and disposing of magistrates. 3. Power over life and death. 4. Making of warre or peace. 5. Highest or last appeals. Where these 5 are, in one or more, there is the state." [7]

---

[6] On this see Bacon, *Preparation toward the Union of the Laws,* in *Works,* xv; Doderidge, in *Parliamentary Debates in 1610,* p. 99.

[7] Sir Walter Raleigh, *The Prince, or Maximes of State, Somers Tracts,* iii, 283. Cowell's *Interpreter* (ed. 1684), title Regalia, says: "The Royal Rights of a King, the Civilians reckon to be six, 1. Power of Judicature. 2. Power of Life and Death. 3. Power of War and Peace. 4. Masterless goods, such as Waifes, Estrayes, &c. 5. Assessments. And 6. Minting of Money." Sir Henry Hobart stated: "In all soveraigne states there are certain *jura majestatis,* that doe designe where *summum imperium* is in the state, i. e. warre and peace, making of lawes, coyne, indenising, calling or dissolving of parliaments, pardoning of offendors, imposing." *Parliamentary Debates in 1610,* p. 90. Virtually all politicists employed such an analysis, even Hobbes and Filmer.

The less sophisticated writers never questioned that the five or six characteristics of sovereignty usually enumerated might be in "one or more." Sir Thomas Smith placed the legislative power in king and Parliament, and the power of judicature in the courts.[8] Hobbes and Filmer, however, reduced sovereignty to the function of law-making. They retained the usual classification of powers as a description of the method by which the sovereign operated; but sovereignty itself was the establishment of law by will. Since law was the will of the sovereign, there could be no division of authority; that would make possible the paradox of conflicting wills in the sovereign. The only possible government was absolute monarchy.

The more moderate theorists agreed that it was possible that all the powers of sovereignty might by the fundamental laws be vested in one man. Such a ruler might or might not be an absolute monarch. He might be circumscribed by law, for to most writers law had an objective existence, and did not depend merely on human will. The classic distinction which Fortescue had drawn between *dominus regalis* and *dominus politicus et regalis* was familiar; and most men considered England *dominium politicum et regale,* a monarchy limited by law and not absolute. This is by no means equivalent to the observation previously made, that Parliament shared the legislative power with the king. It was the law, and not Parliament, that limited the king; not until the Civil War did men erect Parliament into a coordinate authority.

Whether or not the monarch was bound by human law, he was bound by "the law of nature and the law of God." Even Hobbes felt obliged to take account of these forces; he turned them to advantage by insisting that they prescribed and sanctioned the absolutist government he advocated. With most theorists they were an expression of the accepted proposition that government was moral in character, and could not infringe the ultimate moralities.

---

[8] *De Republica Anglorum,* Book II, Chap. 5.

Legislation was not arbitrary will, but was therapeutic, and consequently was unlikely to conflict with the law of nature or the law
of God. It is significant that Philip Hunton uses as a synonym for
"legislative" the word "architectonical"; the nature of legislation
was to rectify, to make perfect, and not to pervert.[9] King James
expressed the same idea: "in all Parliaments, the King must have
a special Care to make good Laws; for it is true, *Ex malis moribus
bonae leges oriuntur*: for the elder the world grows, Men become
more crafty and sinful, and some the more wise; and for new
Crimes we must needs have new Laws."[10] Thomas Hobbes, perhaps without due consideration, said that the sovereign's command
was not legislative in character, and consequently not lawful, if
it were retroactive, or discriminatory as to persons rather than
general.[11]

But it was certainly possible for the government to contravene
the law of nature or the law of God. Apparently the imposition
of a heretical faith upon the nation would be such a case. The

---

[9] To Hunton an irrational will is "no will intended to be the Law of Soveraignty."
Treatise of Monarchy, Part I, Chap. ii, Sec. 3 (4).

[10] Speech to Parliament, 1621, in [Nicholas,] *Proceedings and Debates in the House
of Commons, 1620-1621* (1766) i, 4 ff.

[11] So if the king command a man to put to death his father, who has previously been
convicted of crime, he need not be obeyed: "we are to consider whether that Command
were one of his Laws; for by disobeying Kings, we mean the disobeying of his Laws;
Laws, those his Laws that were made before they were applied to any particular Person:
for the King, (though he is sometimes considered as a Father of Children, and a Master
of Domestic Servants,) yet he commands the People in general never but by a precedent
Law, and as a politic, not a natural person. And, if such a command as you speak of were
contrived into a general Law, (which, however, never was, nor ever will be) you would
be bound to obey it. . . ." *Behemoth, English Works* (ed. Molesworth) vi, 227. There is
an admission implicit in Hobbes' argument that the King of England can punish at-
tempted arson: "It is neither treason, nor murder, nor burglary, . . . nor contrary to any
statute. And yet, seeing the common-law is the law of reason, it is a sin, and such a sin
as a man may be accused of, and convicted; and consequently a crime committed of
malice prepensed. Shall he not then be punished for the attempt? I grant you that a judge has
no warrant from any statute-law, common-law, or commission, to appoint the punishment; but surely the King has power to punish him, on this side of life or member, as
he please; and with the assent of Parliament, if not without, to make the crime for the
future capital." *Dialogue of the Common Laws, English Works*, vi, 62. The assumption
that an offense which is already punishable cannot be made capital retroactively is another
indication of the view that *ex post facto* legislation is not genuine law. (The requirement
of the concurrence of Parliament to make the crime capital is merely a constitutional
rule. *Ibid.*, p. 109.)

defenders of political authority took two courses here. One was to insist that the action, despite its ungodly appearance, was lawful because it came from a government established by God. So Hooker considered lawful the statutes of Mary's reign, which returned England to subjection to the papacy, arguing that "our laws made concerning religion, do take originally their essence from the power of the whole realm and church of England, than which nothing can be more consonant unto the law of nature and the will of our Lord Jesus Christ." [12] The other defense was to admit the illegality of the sovereign's act, but to urge upon the subjects their peculiar duty, as Christians, to endure evil.[13] The whole theory of passive obedience illustrates the limitation of lawful power in government; the exhortation to non-resistance admits that an anti-Christian law has no claim to active obedience in its own right, but urges that the Christian is bound, by another and higher law, to submit to oppression. In the ultimate case the theorists of absolutism admitted the limitation of lawful power, and made on behalf of the sovereign a claim of sufferance rather than of right. It was with this uncongenial plaster that Hobbes filled the gap in the nearly impregnable wall of sovereignty he had built about his ruler.[14]

---

[12] *Laws of Ecclesiastical Polity,* Book VIII, Chap. vi, 11.

[13] *Romans,* xiii, 1. George Wither, a Parliamentary captain, justified himself rather ambiguously: "I have been actively or passively obedient to every Government whereunto God hath subjected me. . . . I *neither was* nor *am,* nor *shall be* disobedient to the just commands of any *Governours* or *Government* which these *Nations* desire, and God permits, (though in his wrath) but conscientiously, as I now do, submitted at all times to the *Power in Being,* and visibly enabled to protect me, as I ever thought it my duty, whether they favoured or dis-favoured me. . . ." *Paralellogrammaton* (1662-Spenser Society, 1882) p. 31.

Matthew Hale, though a royalist, accepted a place on the Common Pleas under Cromwell. Bishop Burnet says: "he did deliberate more on the lawfulness of taking a commission from usurpers: but having considered well of this, he came to be of opinion, *That it being absolutely necessary to have justice and property kept up at all times, it was no sin to take a commission from usurpers, if he made no declaration of his acknowledging their authority;* which he never did. He was much urged to accept of it by some eminent men of his own profession, who were of the King's party; as Sir Orlando Bridgeman, and Sir Geoffrey Palmer; and was also satisfied concerning the lawfulness of it, by the resolution of some famous divines, in particular Dr. Sheldon and Dr. Henchman, who were afterwards promoted to the fees of Canterbury and London." Burnet, *Life of Hale* (1806) p. 28.

[14] See *Leviathan,* Part III, Chap. 43.

There was in England no serious opposition to the doctrine of passive obedience until the Civil War. But there was in England a settled body of opinion not greatly at variance with the philosophy of the Jesuits and the continental and Scotch Calvinists, who had long preached resistance and even tyrannicide. The insistence that the king and state were distinct, that there could be no king without a people but there might be a people without a king, had indeed a better basis in England than in France. The author of the *Vindiciae* felt obliged to unify the people of France with a covenant to God, and to employ the analogy to the headless nation of Israel, in order to establish the independent existence of the state. But the English had long possessed a sense of the reality of the nation. The long history of Parliament, and above all the possession of a genuine national law, bound England into a nation without regard to the vicissitudes of rule. There was before the Civil War no developed theory that the king shared his power with the people, but the elements of such a theory were at hand. Governor and governed were set apart; the contract theory of the origin of the state already existed. To adopt a theory of revolution meant substituting the sovereignty of will for the sovereignty of law, but this change could easily be concealed. Institutionally, moreover, England was prepared for the change, for there existed in Parliament not merely the minor magistrate whom Calvin authorized to resist the illegal demands of the prince, but an agency which could plausibly claim to represent the kingdom and consequently could assert that the "higher powers" to whom obedience was due meant Parliament.

A fundamental difference between the royalist or naturalist school of thought and the Parliamentary or legalist is illustrated by the variance of their conceptions of the function of law. To King James or Filmer, for example, law existed in order to enable the king to discharge his patriarchal duty of safeguarding the community. It did not consist, therefore, of rules by which right was determined, but of an adaptation and amelioration of rules. The equity of just dealing was the significant feature of law. It was well to have settled rules, and to abide by them in ordinary cases, because that had obvious social advantages; but in the unusual case the king was obliged to ignore set rules and do justice according to his conscience.

The legalists, on the other hand, were likely to regard right simply as the enforcement of law. On a higher plane, they insisted upon a strict, abstract justice which should never yield to circumstance or human need. This was thoroughly consistent with their Puritan heritage. The extreme Protestants seem to have regarded this rigid justice as the highest of values. It was one of the German Protestants of the sixteenth century who first said, *Fiat justitia et pereat mundus.* William Prynne printed on the title-page of his *New Wandering Blazing Stars, Fiat justitia, ruat coelum;* and George Wither wrote

> Fiat justitia, ruat Coelum:
> Rather than Justice should be made a scorn,
> Let all the Planets from their Sphears be torn.[15]

This dogmatic adherence to a single code is in striking contrast with King James' frequent warning that *summum jus* might be *summa injuria.*

It would be unwise, however, to attribute the whole of the Parliamentary aversion to equity to such lofty sentiments. Part of it, no doubt, came from the professional jealousy between the common law courts and the Chancery, and from the distrust of a court process immediately amenable to the king's will. Another ground

---

[15] *Speculum Speculativum,* title-page.

Too much importance can easily be attached to these popular tags. The Duke of Richmond, cousin of Charles I, in defending himself from the accusations of the House of Commons in 1642, asserted "Magna est veritas et prevalebit," and aspired "Regnet justitia et ruat Coelum."

The declaration of Lord Mansfield on the duty of judges should be quoted in conjunction with these Puritan writers. "The constitution does not allow reasons of state to influence our judgments: God forbid that it should: We must not regard political consequences; how formidable soever they might be: if rebellion was the certain consequence, we are bound to say 'fiat justitia, ruat coelum'." Rex v. Wilkes, 4 Burrows 2562 (1768).

was quaintly expressed by Selden when he said, "Equity is a Roguish thing, for Law we have a measure, know what to trust too, Equity is according to the Conscience of him that is Chancellor, and as it is larger or narrower so is equity."[16] As we shall see later, the Parliamentarians were obliged in the stress of civil war to abandon their allegiance to immutable law, and to employ the royalist argument of reason of state, but reason of state consorted ill with their general attitude, and Selden at least never compromised with his early beliefs.

II

There was before the Civil War very little necessity for speculation as to the ultimate source of political authority. In so far as there was an inherited theory, it was twofold. There had been no inconsistency, in the eyes of the middle ages, in attributing the power of rulers to the people and also to God. Hooker continued this tradition. "Original influence of power from the body into the king, is the cause of the king's dependency in power upon the body."[17] This was a natural corollary from the contract theory, but it went hand in hand with rule by divine right. "Unto kings by human right, honour by very divine right, is due. . . . And therefore of what kind soever the means be whereby governors are lawfully advanced unto their seats, as we by the law of God stand bound meekly to acknowledge them for God's lieutenants, and to confess their power his, so they by the same law are both authorized and required to use that power as far as it may be in any sort available to his honour."[18]

To most Englishmen at the opening of the seventeenth century the rather exotic contract doctrine was probably unfamiliar; they would have rested the king's right to rule on God and the law. This

---

[16] *Table Talk* (ed. Pollock) p. 43.
[17] *Laws*, Book VIII, Chap. ii, 9.
[18] *Ibid.*, Book VIII, Chap. ii, 6.

was in effect what Hooker did, for with Hooker, as later with Edmund Burke, the contract was merely a device for initiating the law. The law established the office of kingship, and conferred it upon the rightful claimant; God sanctified his rule.

Even James admitted that he came to the throne by the common law of England.[19] The law of succession was the law of real property. Coke, however, declared that it was possible for the king, with the consent of Parliament, to nominate his successor by will. He cited the case of Henry VIII, which was not a welcome precedent at that time. King James had come to the throne in defiance of two acts of Parliament and Henry's will; his only claim was the right of strict hereditary succession. Not only James, but the whole kingdom was committed to the theory of divine, unalterable right to the succession. Coke's recalcitrancy can be explained, perhaps, by his reluctance to abandon any precedent; perhaps his devotion to Parliament led him to prize this particular precedent; perhaps he realized that the theory of hereditary succession could not possibly square with English history. But his opinion was very unpopular: most men considered that only the law of primogeniture could govern succession to the throne.

This, however, leaves unresolved the question of the king's relation to God. In an inoffensive way the king had always claimed to rule by divine right, for only God, as Bracton said, can make an heir. The princes of Europe since Pepin had used the title *Rex Dei gratia,* and kingship was not the only office that was so held. Bishops and other dignitaries in the middle ages had likewise signed themselves *Dei gratia:* by the appointed method of election or choice, they had acquired a rule which God sanctified.[20]

This sort of divine rule is merely an honorific title. It character-

---

[19] "His Majestie said further that for his Kingdome he was beholden to noe elective power, neither doth he depend upon any popular applause; and yet he doth acknowledge that, though he did derive his tytle from the loynes of his ancestors; yet the lawe did set the crowne upon his head, and he is a Kinge by the comon lawe of the land." *Parliamentary Debates in 1610,* p. 24.

[20] George St. Amand, *Legislative Power of England* (1725).

izes the rule, but does not vest it with any specific power. Nor does the proposition for which Hooker stood purport to convey any special power to the prince. It merely states that the power which the law has vested in the prince is a moral rule, disobedience to which would be a sin. For all the talk of "God's lieutenants," there is no real claim of viceregency. God approved of kings, as of republican magistrates, but did not communicate to them his own power. Political power had originally come from the people, and was now conferred and confined by law.

This moderate and secular view brings God into no great prominence in political theory. He is an auxiliary called upon to reinforce a system which is by itself quite complete. The need for such reenforcement resulted from the arguments of Goodman and Bellarmine and Mariana and Buchanan, those "seedsmen of rebellion," as Hooker called them.

These writers, Calvinists and Catholics, represent a genuine and purposeful intrusion of God into politics. They argued that God had conferred power upon kings in order that they might promote the work of His Church, and that kings who failed to discharge this trust were to be called to account by the spiritual authority. Both the Calvinists and the Jesuits were very active on the continent, and the Calvinists dominated Scotland as well, but neither group succeeded in altering the essentially secular character of English thought. Even English Calvinists like William Prynne argued in terms of national law and the rights of Parliament rather than the moral accountability of the prince.

Nevertheless, this school of thought posed a problem which Englishmen were compelled to answer. An answer in terms of national law was not adequate, for the Calvinists and the Jesuits relied upon nothing less than divine law. It was necessary to argue that morality forbade subjects to rebel against a king. One argument employed by the champions of kings was the familiar counsel of Romans xiii, to submit "not only for wrath, but also for conscience' sake." This was more directly a duty of Christians than of subjects. The other argument, much more vague, was that the king derived his "right" from God alone, and consequently was accountable only to God. There is a wide range of meaning in this proposition. To Hooker, as we have seen, it meant only that God sanctified political office. The right, not the power, was divine. Consequently divine law made no prescription as to the extent of royal power; that was an affair of national law. If the king violated national law, his actions were illegal; nevertheless, Christians must submit to his misrule. Later royalist churchmen made the same claims, much more shrilly, with lavish citation of Scripture, but without substantially extending Hooker's argument. Sibthorpe's sermon on *Apostolic Obedience,* which so rankled the House of Commons, was merely a more propagandist statement of Hooker's position. Only Roger Manwaring appears to have established a scheme in which full meaning is given to the idea that kings are "God's lieutenants." In his *Religion and Allegiance*[21] Manwaring argued that the authority of kings was a branch of God's authority, communicated directly by Him. As we shall see, he built up a philosophy of unitary rule in which all order and all command derived immediately from the divine fountain head. Since the king's power was conferred by God, it could not be limited by any human law. In other theorists the counsel of nonresistance perhaps makes divine right a creed of practical absolutism; but only in Manwaring is it a creed of theoretical absolutism.

Somewhere between Hooker and Manwaring the bulk of royalist argument is to be distributed. The claim of divine right was by no means confined to churchmen; King James used it lavishly, and other secular writers more sparingly. But it seems certain that they used it as a means of characterizing the position of the prince, rather than describing his power. The orthodox theory of sov-

---

[21] Two sermons delivered before Charles I in 1627. On Manwaring see Chapter VI, *infra.*

ereignty made political power a purely natural phenomenon, the capacity to draw order out of anarchy by the institution of command. This capacity was part of the natural order of things, like the analogous function of the king-bee in the hive, the patriarch in his family, the devil among the legions of hell. It was attributable to God only in that God was the author of the universe. Command was not supernatural, and the universe was not one great monarchy. Rather, command was natural, and was plural. Indeed, it might be said that the command of God Himself was but one among many examples of a great law of nature which underlay even His empire.

This naturalistic theory is plain Aristotelianism, and Aristotelianism in the hands of Marsiglio had already proved its strength as a weapon for combating the papacy. It seems odd that the royalist writers did not employ it for that purpose, but instead added to their store of arguments the incongruous claim of divine right. But Marsiglio had the great advantage over James of being an atheist; James could not have brought himself to the point of declaring the entire natural universe none of God's affair. Moreover, Scripture carried much more weight than Aristotle in England in the seventeenth century, and had more propaganda value. And, finally, only James and Filmer conspicuously busied themselves with talk of divine right: the ordinary secular royalist writers did not address themselves to the Calvinists or the Jesuits, and hence needed no theological claims.

Figgis has brilliantly established the secular character of Filmer's thought.[22] With James it is a question of emphasis: if one attributes most weight to his writings against Bellarmine, his politics was essentially theological; if one takes other works as representative, he appears an Aristotelian.[23] But even James has nothing resembling Manwaring's assertion that kings are immediately de-

---

[22] *Divine Right of Kings*, Chap. 7.
[23] See the discussion of James in Chapter VI, *infra*.

pendent upon God. It seems important to distinguish sharply three positions: the naturalism of ordinary royalist thought; the "divine right" of Hooker; and the "divine power" of Manwaring. In dealing with any particular theorist it is often difficult or impossible to tell exactly what he means when he is calling the king God's lieutenant—whether he is merely condemning rebellion, with Hooker, or is preaching absolutism with Manwaring. There is little definite evidence that Manwaring's extreme views were widely accepted, even within the Church. Henry Valentine, in a sermon before King Charles in 1639, set forth an incomplete version of Manwaring's scheme.[24] There seems an echo also in the Canons of 1640,[25] which Laud drove through a reluctant Synod:

> The most high and sacred order of Kings is of divine right, being an ordinance of God himself, founded in the prime laws of nature, and clearly established by express texts both of the Old and New Testaments. A supreme power is given to this most excellent order by God Himself in the Scriptures, which is, That Kings should rule and command in their several dominions all persons of what rank or estate soever, whether ecclesiastical or civil, and that they should restrain and punish with the temporal sword all stubborn and wicked doers.

But Manwaring certainly had no large following within the Church, and with the Civil War it became unnecessary, as it had always been inadvisable, for churchmen to employ his argument. The assumption of power by Parliament made it possible for the royalists to rest on the safer ground of constitutional law; consequently, there came a great moderation of tone in royalist argument. The Church confined itself to the well-worn plea for passive obedience, which did not necessarily carry with it any assumption of divine or even legal right on the part of the sovereign. This duty of obedience was not a political theory, but a theological theory. Robert Sanderson, the Bishop of Lincoln, who in 1660 wrote an

---

[24] *God Save the King.* See the quotations from this sermon on p. 8, *supra.*
[25] *Constitutions and Canons Ecclesiasticall,* in Laud's *Works* (Library of Anglo-Catholic Theology, 1853) v, 613.

introduction to Bishop Ussher's *Power Communicated By God to the Prince, and the Obedience Required of the Subject,* freely conceded the point.[26]

> For human laws cannot be the adequate measure of moral duty in the judgment of any reasonable man (for atheists, though masters of never so much reason, I reckon not as reasonable men), the laws being finite and fixed, but the circumstances of men's actions, on which their lawfulness and unlawfulness chiefly depend, various and infinite. The laws allow (and of necessity so must) many things to be done, which an honest man would be loath to do; and affordeth sundry advantages, which one that feareth God, and maketh conscious of his ways, ought not to take.

Sometimes, indeed, one seems to see in the badly written and badly printed little tracts on the duty of obedience which flooded England during the Civil War disjointed fragments of Manwaring's great scheme, so that one might conjecture, as naturalists do from the remains in the stomachs of predatory animals, that Manwaring has been ingested and partly digested. But nothing like the original plan stands out. The political expediency of avoiding any such grandiose claims when the king might securely rest on arguments more generally acceptable may account for this; at any rate, Manwaring is the only reputable royalist theorist to stand completely and unmistakably for the proposition that the authority of the king was divine authority infused into him by God.

---

[26] Ussher's *Works* (1864) xi, 242.

CHAPTER IV

THE LEGAL THEORY OF THE CONSTITUTION

I. *The common law; law of state.*

II. *The natural and political capacities of the king; the pre-rogatives absolute and ordinary, indisputable and dis-putable, inseparable and separable; the Parliamentary repudiation of the absolute prerogative.*

III. *The characters of Parliament; the legislative power of Parliament; limits of legislative power; confusion of legislation and adjudication.*

I

THE trust theory of government to which the Civil Wars gave birth has taken such firm root that even today we are inclined to think of a constitution as an instrument conferring powers upon a government. If this be the meaning of the word constitution, there was no theory of the constitution in the early seventeenth century. Clearly the royalist writers had no such theory, for this definition argues that the authority of government is derivative. Filmer and Hayward contended that authority was natural, and innate in the king; and Manwaring, who considered the king's authority to be derivative, derived it from God and no "ordinance of man." Their opponents, the common lawyers and the Parliament, did indeed ground the government on laws; but they had no notion of a "constitution." The term appears in almost its present sense in some of the Civil War writings, but it was not until after the Glorious Revolution that this specialized meaning became current. The seventeenth century thought of its principles of government in the plural: there were "fundamental laws," there were "constitutions"; but there was no fundamental law, no constitution. Even Cromwell, acting under an Instrument of Government, thought that in every government "some things are Fundamentals"; and the colonists in Connecticut drafting a constitution described it as "Fundamental Orders."

This is partly because the idea of systematic law did not exist. In the seventeenth century the whole body of the law was plural; it was a congeries of isolated and unrelated rules. This is well illustrated by the manner in which legal treatises were written: they were ordinarily in the form of dictionaries or glosses. But the lack of a systematic body of public laws is also to be attributed to the fact that no clear notion of public law existed. It has already been said that the "fundamental laws" were approved as such because experience had demonstrated their value rather than because a formal analysis of government showed them to possess the mechanical qualifications of modern public law. Only in the early years of the Civil War did men begin to think analytically of their principles of government.

But although the earlier period offers no self-conscious constitutional theory, it does offer independent ideas on several topics which contribute to constitutional theory. It is possible to extract from the laws of the land those dealing with the institutions of government; and although this selection does violence to the perspective and emphasis of the early seventeenth century, the data thus obtained will still be valid as an expression of the legal opinion of the period.

It will be by no means a unanimous opinion. Before the various issues between the king and the courts and Parliament arose, opinion was very vague; and after they arose it was divided. There was a difference of opinion even on the first question, as to what law was basic in the kingdom. This was the most important question of all. If the common law was the sole source of the authority of the king, it followed that the king was, outside the privileges granted him by the common law, completely powerless: he could not lay impositions on imports, or imprison subjects in violation of Magna Carta. But if it were the common law that was limited, and not the king; if the prohibitions of the common law bound the king only within the realm, and only in cases cognizable by the common law, then the king in levying impositions or in arresting for reason of state was acting by virtue of an authority granted by the "Civil Law . . . which in the Point of Conjunction of Nations, should bear a great Sway, it being the Law of Nations." [1]

It was possible to argue that the common law was limited in scope without adopting the royalist philosophy of government. It was well known that other laws than the common law existed in England: Coke in his treatise on Littleton listed fifteen kinds of law, of which common law was fourth and statute law fifth. But the common lawyers insisted that the common law was basic, and controlled the provinces of all other laws. The courts of common law succeeded in enforcing this view with considerable success; over a period of years they make good their claim to determine the jurisdiction of the ecclesiastical courts, the Court of Requests, and the High Commission. In the dispute between Coke and Ellesmere over the Chancery jurisdiction, however, James asserted the right which the civil law gave to princes: "that in any case wherein the Law is thought not to be cleared . . . then in such a question wherein no positive Law is resolute, *Rex est judex;* for he is *lex loquens,* and is to supply the Law where the Law wants. . . ." [2]

---

[1] James to Parliament, 1606. *Commons Journal,* i, 361.

[2] *Ibid.* This was the opinion of Ellesmere as well: "So as now if this question seem difficult, that neither direct law, nor Examples & Precedents, nor application of like cases, nor discourse of reason, nor the grave opinion of the learned and reverend Judges, can resolve it, here is a true and certen Rule; how both by the Civile Lawe, and by the ancient Common lawe of England it may and ought to be decided: That is, by sentence of the most religious, learned, and judicious king that ever this kingdome or Iland had." *Speech of*

The question is substantially that disputed between the Commons and the Lords in 1628, concerning the *lex terrae* clause of Magna Carta and arrests made in violation of the common law.[3]

And thereupon M. Serjeant Ashley offered an interpretation of them thus; namely, that there were divers Laws of this Realm; as the Common Law; the Law of the Chancery; the Ecclesiastical Law; the Law of Admiralty or Marine Law; the Law of Merchants; the Martial Law; and the Law of State; and that these words (per legem terrae) do extend to all those laws.

To this it was answered that we read of no law of State, and that none of the laws can be meant there, save the Common, which is the principal and general Law, and is always understood by way of *Excellency*, when mention is made of the *Law* of the Land generally; and that though each of the other Laws which are admitted into this kingdom by Custom or Act of Parliament, may justly be called a Law of the Land; yet none of them can have that preheminency to be stiled the Law of the Land; and no Statute, Law-book or other authority printed or unprinted could be shewed to prove that the Law of the Land, being generally mentioned, was ever intended of other Law than the Common Law . . . but it standeth with the Rule of other legal expositions, that *per legem terrae* must be meant the Common Law, by which the general and universal Law by which men hold their Inheritances. . . .

It was of course possible to believe in a common law prerogative which conferred substantially the same rights upon the king as did the law of state. This in fact seems to have been a very general position before 1621. But when the consequences of this view were finally realized, after the arrests and forced loans of the 1620's, the common law was contracted sharply: it no longer contained principles of government, but became merely "the general and universal Law by which men hold their Inheritances."

II

The distinction which Coke drew between the king and the crown in Calvin's Case has already been referred to. The extent

---

the Lord Chancellor of England, in the Eschequer Chamber, touching the Post-Nati (London, 1609) p. 108.

[3] *Lords Journal,* iii, 758. The quotation is from *Cottoni Posthuma* (1672) p. 245. Ashley's argument is given on p. 79, *infra.*

and significance of this distinction at the time it was made were not at all clear. It was pregnant with possibilities, which the Long Parliament was not slow to realize. The most revealing thing about its use in 1607 is the fact that it was forced upon the court by the attorneys for the defense, and that the decision itself was a not quite successful evasion of it. The plaintiff argued that a Scotch subject born after James' accession to the throne of England, being under the same allegiance as the English, was entitled to sue for English lands in the English courts. This attributed a significance to the person of the king which went beyond the issues of the particular case. The defense argued that James was in effect two kings, the king of Scotland and the king of England; the fact that he occupied two thrones did not in any way unite the crowns, the laws, or the kingdoms. This smacked of what Coke called the "damnable and damned opinion" of "Spencer's Case"—the doctrine that "Homage and oath of allegiance is more by reason of the crown than by reason of the king's person and is more bound to the crown than the person ... wherefore if the king by chance be not guided by reason, in the right of the crown, his lieges are bound by oath made to the crown to guide the king and the estate of the crown back again by reason, and otherwise the oath would not be kept."[4] The judges accepted the division of the crowns, and the distinction between the king and the crown, but insisted that allegiance "was due to the natural person of the king, which is ever accompanied with the politick capacity ... and it is not due to the politick capacity only."[5] Consequently the Scot could maintain his suit.

---

[4] *Statutes of the Realm*, i, 82.

[5] Coke's opinion in Calvin's Case, *Howell's State Trials*, ii, 624. This distinction dates from the Case of the Duchy of Lancaster, Plowden, 212. Perhaps Ellesmere's statement is the best: "But in this new learning, there is one part of it so strange, and of so dangerous consequent, as I may not let it pass, *viz.* that the king is as a king divided in himselfe; and so as two kinges of two several kingdomes; and that there be severall allegeances, and several subjections due unto him respectively in regarde of his severall kingdomes, the one not participating with the other.

"This is a dangerous distinction between the King and the Crowne, and between the

This attachment of allegiance to the person rather than the office of the king was perhaps merely a device to escape the doctrine of "Spencer's Case." The eagerness of the judges to support James' claim that there was a union of thrones doubtless assisted them to their decision. But other theorists than lawyers attached a sanctity to the person of the king which may indicate that they accepted the legal principle of personal allegiance. Perhaps if Cromwell met the king in battle he would fire his pistol at him, but most of the publicists of his party, even while advocating resistance to the king, insisted that it was improper to injure him in person. That confirmed republican Algernon Sidney refused to sit on the High Court of Justice which tried Charles I, because, although he believed it proper to depose the king, he thought it wrong to punish him.

It can also be said that the distinction between the personal and public capacities of the king was thoroughly accepted in Parliament. Of course James, who believed that political authority derived from the person of the king, rejected the distinction, and argued that his accession to the throne of England had united the crowns of the two kingdoms, and had brought into existence the new realm of "Great Britain." But speakers debating the Union in the House of Commons insisted *"Rex Angliae, Rex Scotiae— Reges,"* [6] and, echoing Calvin's Case, *"Legiancia, a ligo; legis, a legendo"* [7]—the king's personal rights came from another source and were distinct from those which the law placed in the crown.

King and the Kingdome: It reacheth too farre; I wish every good subject to beware of it. It was never taught, but either by traitors, as in *Spencers* Bill in Ed. 2. time. . . .

"This bond of Allegiance whereof we dispute, is *Vinculum fidei;* it bindeth the soule and conscience of every subject, severally and respectively, to bee faithfull and obedient to the King: And as a Soule or Conscience cannot be framed by Policie; so Faith and Allegiance cannot be framed by policie, nor put into a politike body. . . .

"Now then, since there is but one king, and soveraigne to whom this faith and allegiance is due by al his loyal subjects of *England* and *Scotland,* can any humane policie divide this one King, and make him two kings?" *Speech of the Lord Chancellor of England, in the Eschequer Chamber, touching the Post-Nati* (London, 1609) p. 99 ff.

[6] See, for example, *Commons Journal,* i, 1015.

[7] *Commons Journal,* i, 1019.

"Concerning the royal person there is to be considered 1) the multiplicity of it, for first it is both lay and clergy having jurisdiction over both. Then it is a corporation as some call it. I should rather call it a perpetual person, because it never dieth. But if it must be a corporation let it be a successive corporation. Lastly it is a single person, being he is a man, and in such capacity he may take things and not annex them to the crown."[8]

The king, that is, is Supreme Governor of the Church, and has by his prerogative "the supreme and sovereign authority in all causes ecclesiastical."[9] This assertion reaches at least to Henry VIII. The idea of the king as a corporation is somewhat more recent; indeed, Maitland says that "I strongly suspect that Coke himself was still living when men first called the king a corporation sole."[10] The corporation sole had been developed in the preceding century to cover the case of parsons, who acquired by virtue of office the glebe attached to the parish, and was easily extended to the king, who came into rights attached to his office.[11] For it was, presumably, the corporation sole that had a "politick capacity." The corporate character of the king was extremely useful also in establishing the deathlessness of the king; it is perhaps surprising that only Forsett among the political theorists employed this legal device.[12]

In his political capacity the king possessed so many of the powers which the civil lawyers ascribed to the complete sovereign that it is not surprising to find a civilian like Cowell claiming that the king of England was a genuine sovereign. He had the powers

---

[8] "A discourse concerning the prerogative of the Crown," in the hand of William Camden, Stowe Mss., 237.

[9] "Treatise on the King's Prerogative," Harleian Mss., 5220, attributed to Sir John Doderidge.

[10] "The Corporation Sole," *Selected Essays*, p. 81.

[11] *Ibid*.

[12] "In his personal respects hee is as one man, single and individuall, yet as in the right of Soveraigntie, he gayneth the Appellation and capacities of a corporation: In his personall respects death maketh an end of his life and glorie all at once, but soveraigntie never faileth." *A Comparative Discourse of the Bodies Natural and Politique* (London, 1606) p. 33.

of coinage, of war and peace, and of appointment of magistrates; the most conspicuous exception to his complete authority was the legislative power, which he shared with Parliament. James, in describing to the Spanish ambassador the paramountcy of his position, stopped in confusion when he touched on Parliament; the ambassador tactfully pointed out that Parliament was convened and dissolved at the king's pleasure, and James gratefully agreed.

But the English lawyers did not ordinarily think of the king as exercising abstract political powers defined by the civil law; more congenial to them was the term "prerogative." The prerogative was a miscellaneous group of property rights, such as the ownership of the swans on the river Thames and the feudal incidents enumerated in the medieval statute *De Prerogativa Regis*. But the prerogative was also a group of political rights, just as heterogeneous, and, like the private property rights of the king, rooted in the common law of the land. At least, Coke said "the King has no prerogative but that which the law of the land allows him."[13] But here we encounter the same problem as before. To Coke the law of the land was the common law: the law which defined the rights of subjects was also the law which gave power over subjects to the king. But the royalist lawyers rested the royal power on quite another basis. Chief Baron Fleming said in Bate's Case:[14]

The King's power is double, ordinary and absolute, and they have several laws and ends. That of the ordinary is for the profit of particular subjects, for the execution of civil justice, the determining of *meum;* and this is exercised by equity and justice in ordinary courts, and by the civilians is nominated *jus privatum,* and with us common law; and these laws cannot be changed without parliament. . . . The absolute power of the King is not that which is converted or executed to private use, to the benefit of any particular person, but is only that which is applied to the general benefit of the people, and is *salus populi;* as the people is the body, and the King the head; and this power is not guided by the rules which direct only at

---

[13] Case of Proclamations, 12 Reports 74 (1610).
[14] *Howell's State Trials,* ii, 30 (1606).

the common law, and is most properly named policy and government; and as the constitution of this body varieth with the time, so varieth this abso-lute law, according to the wisdom of the King, for the common good; and these being general rules, and true as they are, all things done within these rules are lawful.

The ordinary power, then, was the power to govern by rules of private law, and the ordinary prerogative consisted of the private rights of the king. The absolute prerogative was the power to act outside the common law for reason of state; or, in the hands of some jurists, it comprised the half-dozen powers which we have seen enumerated as the elements of sovereignty.[15]

Bacon appears to have originated the characterization of disput-able and indisputable; the ordinary prerogative might be disputed in the courts, but the absolute prerogative, like "political questions" in American constitutional law, might not be disputed. So he said in his *View of the Differences in Question Betwixt the King's Bench and the Council in the Marches:*[16] "though other preroga-tives by which he [the king] claymeth any matter of revenue, or other right pleadable in his ordinary courts of justice, may be there

---

[15] See Yelverton's speech, *Parliamentary Debates in 1610* (Camden Society, ed. Gardiner) p. 87, and especially see Crawley's judgment in Hampden's Case: "That in these cases, of necessity and danger, the king, jure gentium, may charge the subject, without his consent in parliament, by his regal prerogative; for in the king there are two kinds of prerogatives, *regale et legale,* which concern his person, lands and goods.

"Now for the prerogatives royal of a monarch, they may be resembled to a sphere; the *primus motor* is the king. It is observed, that every planet but one hath a little orb by itself, that moveth in its petty compass: So the center is the commonwealth, the king is the first mover. I will repeat some of these prerogatives, for they are by all laws, and by our laws. The first regal prerogative is this, that containeth all the rest, that the king may give laws to his subjects: and this does not detract from him, when he doth it in parliament. 2. To make peace and war, 19. Ed. 4, 6. 3. To create supreme magistrates. 4. That the last appeal be to the king. 5. To pardon offences. 6. To coin money. 7. To have allegiance, fealty, and homage. And, 8. To impose taxes, without common consent in parliament. These are but the principal, and there are many more of them, and al-lowed by law." *Howell's State Trials,* iii, 1083.

[16] Spedding, *Bacon's Letters and Life,* iii, 371. In the Parliament of 1610 Bacon argued that the king might inhibit debate on "an essentiall thinge which concerned the preroga-tive and power of the Crowne," and that upon receiving such an inhibition the House had always desisted from discussion; if however the matter of prerogative involved the right or interest of subjects, the House should inform the king of its liberties, and pro-ceed. *Parliamentary Debates in 1610,* p. 38. But see the resolution of the Commons, *Com-mons Journal,* i, 431.

disputed, yet his sovereign power, which no judge can censure, is not of that nature; and therefore whatsoever partaketh or dependeth thereon, being matter of government and not of law, must be left to his managing by his council of state." It seems highly probable that James learned from Bacon the doctrine which he delivered in the Case of Commendams:[17] "that his Majesty had a doble prerogative, whereof the one was ordinary, and had relation to his private interrest, which mought bee, and was, every day disputed in Westminster Hall. The other was of a hiegher nature, referringe to his supreame and imperiall power and sovereigntie, which ought not to be disputed or handled in vulgar argument."

This was not an extravagant claim made by James alone; it was orthodox law until the third decade of the century.[18] The royalist lawyers, to be sure, grounded the absolute or indisputable prerogative on law of state, but as late as 1621 Sir Edward Coke found the same distinction in the common law: "I will not examine the Kinges Prerogative. There is a Prerogative disputable and a Prerogative indisputable, as to make warre and Peace; the other concernes *meum et tuum* and are bounded by Lawe." [19] And in the same Parliament Coke twice affirmed that the king might for reason of state imprison without cause shown.[20] And William Hakewill, as good a Parliamentarian as Coke and perhaps a more acute judge of political issues, conceded that "by his absolute

---

[17] *Acts of the Privy Council, 1615-1616*, p. 595, 602. In his speech in the Star Chamber in 1616 James told the judges: "I desire you to give me no more right in my private Prerogative, then you give to any Subject; and therein I will be acquiescent: as for the absolute Prerogative of the Crowne, that is no Subject for the tongue of a Lawyer, nor is lawful to be disputed." *Political Works* (ed. McIlwain) p. 333.

[18] See, in addition to the other citations, the Doderidge Ms., *supra*, and the Case of Whitelocke and Mansell, *Acts of the Privy Council, 1613-1614*, p. 211 ff.

[19] "Pym Diary," *Commons Debates, 1621* (ed. Notestein, Relf and Simpson) iv, 79. Sir Edward Nicholas recorded the speech thus: "There is Prerogative indisputable, and Prerogative disputable. Prerogative indisputable, is that the King hath to make War: Disputable Prerogative is tied to the Laws of *England*, wherein the King also hath divers Prerogatives, as *nullum tempus*, &c." *Proceedings and Debates in the House of Commons, 1620-1621* (1766) i, 65.

[20] Nicholas, *op. cit.*, ii, 25, 109.

authority, the King may commit any one to prison during his pleasure."[21]

There was in fact good common law basis for something very like an indisputable prerogative. In case of invasion the king could call all subjects to arms; he might cause houses to be pulled down to stop a fire or plague.[22] But after 1621 these common law rights were strictly confined to the settled principles of feudal law, and the king was grudgingly conceded the precise measure òf his feudal rights.[23] Magna Carta was made to walk again, and the Petition of Right was forced upon Charles. In 1640 Pym admitted: "I know the king hath a transcendent power in many Cases, whereby by proclamation he may guard against sudden accidents"; but he added significantly, "But that this power should be applyed to countenance Monopolies (the projectors being not content with their private Grants without a Proclamation) is without president."[24] The exercise of the King's transcendent power was to be subjected to the common law test of precedent. Thus was the absolute prerogative reduced to ordinary, and disputable.

Until the Long Parliament another classification of prerogatives was universally accepted: there were separable prerogatives, and there were inseparable. The separable prerogatives, again, were private rights of the king, as the right of wardship, which could be surrendered; the inseparable were public and inalienable. It was said that the Great Contract would be illegal, because the king could not surrender his prerogatives, and Bacon replied that "it is impossible where the thing is essentiall and inseparable as to judge

---

[21] *Modus tenendi Parliamentum*, p. 90. The quotation is from the edition of 1660.

[22] These precedents were extensively debated in the Parliament of 1610. See *Parliamentary Debates in 1610*.

[23] Before he set out to quell the rebellion in Scotland in 1639, Charles questioned the lords about him as to whether they believed themselves obliged to attend him at their own expense. Brooke replied, "I will attend the King's Person wheresoever he goes, but for the charge I leave to his Majestie's pleasure." Saye protested that by law he was not obliged to stir out of his county, but assured Charles that out of his affection for him he would accompany him. *Bibliotheca Regia* (1659) p. 372.

[24] Rushworth, *Historical Collection* (1680) iii, 1135.

or do Justice, but for the King to break up his howse or the like is not impossible, for this being doon he neavertheless remaineth a King as before."[25] Coke wrote that "No act can bind the king from any prerogative which is sole and inseparable to his person, but that he may dispense with it by a *Non obstante,* as a sovereign power to command any of his subjects to serve him for the public weal; and this solely and inseparably is annexed to his person; and this royal power cannot be restrained by any act of Parliament, neither in *thesi,* nor in *hypothesi,* but that the king by his royal prerogative may dispense with it; for upon commandment of the king, and obedience of the subject, doth his government consist."[26] Three such inseparable prerogatives were the power to dispense with statutes, the pardoning power, and the right to purveyance; Coke cited decisions which, he alleged, declared statutes void because they conflicted with one or another of these prerogatives. All of the judges in the Ship-Money Case conceded the existence of prerogatives which could not be taken away by act of Parliament. The reported resolution of the judges that military tenures could not be abolished[27] indicates that the inseparable prerogatives were not exclusively governmental in character, though Parliament in 1607 appears to have believed that they were.

The fertile brain of Bacon contrived a supplementary category which should be noticed. The prerogative of justice was inseparable, but might be entrusted by commission to the king's judges. But no discretionary power could be delegated: "The absolute prerogative which is in Kings according to their private will and

---

[25] *The Parliamentary Diary of Robert Bowyer, 1606-1607* (ed. Willson) p. 65.

"Sir John Boys . . . he observed that diverse thinges belonginge to the crowne the King cannot grant, as to pardon felony, to take my Lande to build castles or forts on etc. but sondry other prerogatives the King may grant and depart with all, as a warde before it fall may be granted by his Majestie." *Ibid.,* p. 74.

[26] Case of Non Obstante, or Dispensing Power, 12 Reports 18. But Coke expressed a different attitude in the Parliament of 1625: he said that the king should not pardon accused priests, and "that this was conformable to ancient statuts, but that a wicked worde of *non obstante* marrs them all." *Debates in the House of Commons in 1625* (Camden Society, ed. Gardiner) p. 118.

[27] See *supra,* p. 33n.

judgement cannot be executed by any Subject, neither is it possible to give such power by Commission, or fit to subject the people to the same." [28] This distinction between delegable and non-delegable prerogatives is borne out by the constitutional rule that the king could grant a commission to approve an act of Parliament which had already been passed, but not one which lacked final form,[29] and by the declaration of the judges that the power to execute the penal statutes could not be delegated.[30]

From one point of view the inseparability of the prerogative means that the governmental structure cannot be drastically altered by any legal course; this of course is incompatible with a theory of legislative sovereignty, but no such theory existed until 1642. From another point of view the inseparable prerogatives are powers of sovereignty which cannot be abolished; and this is reconcilable with a doctrine of sovereignty. Bacon wrote: "And yet if the parliament should enact in the nature of the ancient *lex regia,* that there should be no more parliaments held, but that the king should have the authority of the parliament; this act were good in law, *quia potestas suprema seipsum dissolvere potest, ligare non potest;* for as it is in the power of man to kill a man, but it is not in his power to save him alive and to restrain him from breathing and feeling; so it is in the power of parliament to extinguish or transfer their own authority, but not whilst the authority remains entire, to restrain the functions and exercises of the same authority." [31] Logically the converse should be true, and indeed the Cambridge manuscript of the *Maxims of the Law* stated: "or *e converso,* if the king by Parliament were to enact to alter the state, and to translate it from a monarchy to any other form; both these acts

---

[28] *An explanation what manner of persons those should be, that are to execute the power or Ordinance of the Kings Prerogative,* in *Works,* xii, 390-1.

[29] Clarendon, *History of the Rebellion,* III, 248.

[30] *State Papers Domestic,* Nov. 8, 1604. The letter of the judges is printed in W. H. Price, *The English Patents of Monopoly,* p. 164.

[31] *Maxims of the Law, Regula XIX,* in *Works,* xiv, 253.

were good." [32] But here Bacon's philosophy outruns his law. The inseparable prerogatives are elements of sovereignty, and cannot be extinguished; but they can be transferred to Parliament.[33] The king's loyal attorney-general should never have admitted that.

But whether ordinary or absolute, disputable or indisputable, separable or inseparable, even in 1640 certain critical governmental prerogatives remained in the king. The command of the Great and Privy Seals (and, of course, the signet and the sign manual) gave him the powers of appointment, of arrest, of issuing commissions and patents, of staying execution and of pardoning offenders, of convoking and dissolving Parliament—it put in his hands, in short, most of the governmental machinery of the country, and the right of dealing with it within the precedents to be found in the common law. The refusal of Charles to surrender these prerogatives made it necessary for Parliament to counterfeit the Great Seal, to usurp the appointing power, to perform a hundred acts clearly illegal at common law.

III

The High Court of Parliament possessed a number of characters. It was of course a court, or perhaps three courts, with somewhat ill-defined jurisdictions and privileges. In an analogous capacity it was the king's great council, summoned to advise him on pressing matters. It was also "the representative bodie of the kingdome, by contraction drawne into this center like the sunne taken through a glasse, to enforce the strength and heat of his reflection." [34] This is not a theory of virtual representation, nor a theory of any sort; it is merely the assumption that some kind of identification exists between Parliament and the kingdom. It has been said above that in voting subsidies Parliament regarded itself less as an official taxing authority than as an attorney for the nation making a dona-

---

[32] *Ibid.*, xiv, 253n.
[33] *Cf.* Willoughby, *Nature of the State* (1903) p. 221.
[34] Eliot, *Negotium Posterorum* (ed. Grosart) i, 140.

tion to the king on behalf of the nation. Yet the right of peers to sit in the upper house was a purely private right, and the right of boroughs to send members to the Commons was merely a property right of the individual boroughs; this legalism is not compatible with a genuine idea of representation. The representative character of Parliament was not made the basis of a theory of Parliamentary authority until the development of the doctrine of trusteeship by the Long Parliament.

In the earlier period there was no need for a theory on which to ground the miscellaneous powers of Parliament; Parliament was, as Coke said, "a part of the frame of the common laws." [35] Its rights were derived from and defined by precedent: "presidents are the life and rule of parliaments, no other warrant being for the parliament itself, for the authorities it pretends to, then the extent use & practise, which is drawne out by presidents." [36] In view of this preoccupation with precedents it is not surprising that the description of Parliament as a court was as common as any. Coke told the House of Commons in 1593 that that body "is not a court alone; and yet there are some things wherein this Court is a Court by itself, and other things wherein it is no Court of itself." [37] One of the respects in which it was not a court was in its possession of the legislative power. Much has been written about Coke's description of the legislative power by example: "Daughters and Heirs apparant of a man or woman, may by Act of Parliament inherit during the Life of the Ancestor. It may adjudge an Infant or Minor of full age. To attaint a man of treason after his death. To naturalize a meere Alien, and make him a subject borne. It may bastardize a childe that by law is legitimate. . . . To legitimate one that is illegitimate." [38] It has been argued that Coke wished to

---

[35] Preface to Part Nine of the Reports.

[36] Eliot, *op. cit.*, ii, 99.

[37] D'Ewes, *Journals of All the Parliaments During the Reign of Queen Elizabeth* (1682) p. 515.

[38] *Fourth Institute*, 36.

show the transcendent power of Parliament by citing cases of extreme governmental action—private legislation. It has been argued that he thought of Parliament so narrowly that the possibility of general legislation did not occur to him; he envisaged Parliament as a court employing extraordinary procedure for the solution of purely private problems. In fact he was merely following his usual practice of arguing from precedent. The cases he cites are typical of bills one finds recorded as having their first or second or third reading in the Commons Journal. They are heterogeneous; they have no definite general character and one can classify them only from a preconceived theory of the nature of legislation. Coke had no clear preconceived theory of the nature of legislation, and most of his contemporaries had none. A hundred years later lawyers were still speculating as to whether Parliament could change a man into a woman;[39] it was yet another hundred years before the law abandoned its claim of being any sort of reflection of factual truth, or an expression of intelligence or moral worth, and reconciled itself to being merely the articulation of the irresponsible will of a legal sovereign.

Thus far, however, the lawyers of the early Stuart period anticipated the later theory of law as will: they agreed that Parliament could not pass an irrepealable statute. Bacon argued that a sovereign power cannot bind itself;[40] and Coke expressed the same opinion in less philosophical terms: "Acts against the power of the Parliament subsequent bind not."[41] Wherein, then, was the power of Parliament less than legislative? The lawyers shared the preconceptions of the age, which made Hooker submit the sovereign to the laws of God and nature, made Hunton demand a rational will in his sovereign, made Hobbes require generality and prospectivity in legislation. Members of Parliament were bound

---

[39] Wood v. London, 12 Modern Reports 669, 689 (1701).

[40] *Maxims of the Law, Regula XIX*, in *Works*, xiv.

[41] *Fourth Institute*, 42.

to recognize these moral limitations. Lawyers could recognize them only when the law so dictated. Coke himself did not scruple to declare that a statute might be inoperative. "It appears in our books, that in many cases, the common law will controul acts of Parliament, and sometimes adjudge them to be utterly void: for when an act of Parliament is against common right and reason, or repugnant, or impossible to be performed, the common law will controul it, and adjudge such act to be void." [42] There was abundant authority for the general proposition. Stubbs tells us of the twelfth century enactment, the Assize, that "it is liable to be set aside by the judges where they find it impossible to administer it fairly." [43] In the fourteenth century Edward III and Richard II protested, with indifferent success, that certain acts of Parliament curtailing the prerogative were void. *Doctor and Student,* published in the reign of Henry VIII, declared an act of Parliament contrary to the law of nature to be void. It was commonly believed in the time of Coke that Parliament could not pass an act of divorce, terminating a previously valid marriage: a statute purporting to do that had been passed in the reign of Edward VI, but it had been repealed in the reign of Mary, apparently on the ground that Parliament had exceeded its authority, and the unhappy divorcé, who had remarried, was subject to the charge of bigamy. [44] We have seen that no act of Parliament could strip the king of the regalities essential to his office. Coke himself in Bonham's Case relied upon four common law decisions, of which

---

[42] Bonham's Case, 8 Reports 107, 118 (1610). But it should be pointed out that with a little straining this dictum can be converted from an indorsement of "substantive due process," as it has always been interpreted, to a requirement merely of procedural due process. What Coke denounced was permitting the College of Physicians to be judge in its own case against Bonham; if the dictum is applied to this situation the limitation upon the legislative power becomes merely procedural, as in the case of the inseparable prerogatives.

[43] *Constitutional History of England,* i, 616.

[44] Clifford, *History of Private Bill Legislation,* i, 391. The next legislative divorce was that of Lord Roos in 1670, when a bill was pushed through Parliament to create a precedent for a contemplated divorce of Charles II.

Professor Plucknett says "there was at least one clear and incontestable precedent in his favor." [45]

But there is a distinction, not always recognized, between the rule in the Case Of Non Obstante and the dictum in Bonham's Case. The first proposition, that an act of Parliament unsettling the actual governmental structure in a vital point would be unlawful, no lawyer of his day doubted, and members of Parliament commonly conceded it. The second ruling, that a statute would be void which infringed the "common right" of the subject, to use the language of Bonham's Case, or violated the "law of Nature," as *Doctor and Student* put it, is more doubtful. The general attitude which it represents, that the common law had a higher sanction than statute law, was common enough. It found expression in the legal rule that statutes in derogation of the common law were to be construed strictly; it found more poetic expression in Sir John Davies' Preface to his *Primer Report des Cases et Matters in Ley:* "Therefore as the *lawe of nature,* which the Schoolmen call *Ius commune,* and which is also *Ius non scriptum,* being written only in the heart of man, is better than all the written lawes in the world to make men honest and happy in this life, if they would observe the rules thereof: So the *customary law* of England, which we do likewise call *Ius commune,* as comming neerest to the lawe of *Nature,* which is the root and touchstone of all good lawes, and which is also *Ius non scriptum,* and written onely in the memory of man . . . doth far excell our *written lawes,* namely our Statutes or Acts of Parliament." [46]

But the cases in which judges actually announced that a statute could be invalid for infringing any other portion of the common law than that which guaranteed the integrity of the existing governmental structure are few. It was said in the Case of Proclamations:[47] "9 Hen. 4. an act of parliament was made, that all the

---

[45] "Bonham's Case and Judicial Review," *Harvard Law Review,* xl, 30.
[46] Quoted in Professor McIlwain's *Growth of Political Thought in the West,* p. 365.
[47] 12 Reports 74.

Irish people should depart the realm, and go into Ireland before the feast of the Nativity of the Blessed Lady, upon pain of death, which was absolutely *in terrorem,* and was utterly against the law." And in 1614 Justice Hobart stated that "an act of Parliament made against Natural Equity, as to make a Man Judge in his own Cause, is void in itself, for *Jura Naturae sunt immutabilia* and they are *leges legum.*" [48] It is interesting to note that in Massachusetts in 1657 a tax to build a manse for the minister was held illegal as a taking of property for private use: "the fundamental law which God and nature have given to the people cannot be infringed. The right of property is such a fundamental right. In this case the goods of one man were given to another without the former's consent. This resolve of the town being against the fundamental law is therefore void, and the taking was not justifiable." [49]

Certainly there was less agreement on Coke's proposition that a statute was void if it conflicted with natural law than on the principle that a statute unsettling the governmental structure was void. Bacon, who agreed with Coke that the Sheriff of Northumberland's Case established (as apparently it did not) [50] that the dispensing power could not be curtailed by statute, charged the wider language of the dictum in Bonham's Case against Coke as one of the five erroneous propositions for which, ostensibly, he was removed from the bench. And Lord Chancellor Ellesmere, in investing Coke's successor, Sir Henry Montague, admonished him: "Remember Sir Edward Mountague your worthy Grandfather. . . . He never made teste Edwardo Mountague to justle with teste meipso, but knew that the Kings writ, test meipso, was his warrant to sit in this place. . . . He challenged not power for the Judges of this Court to correct all misdemeanors as well extra-

---

[48] Day v. Savadge, Hobart, 85, 87.

[49] Quoted in Paul S. Reinsch, *English Common Law in the Early American Colonies* (Univ. of Wis. Bulletin) p. 16, reprinted in *Select Essays in Anglo-American Legal History,* i, 367.

[50] Plucknett, *op. cit.,* p. 46.

judicial as judicial, nor to have power to judge Statutes and Acts of Parliament to be void, if they conceived them to be against common right and reason; but left the King and the Parliament to judge what was common right and reason. I speak not of impossibilities or direct repugnances."[51] And Montague replied, "I will not be busie in stirring questions, especially of Jurisdictions."[52] Indeed, even Coke, though he sturdily refused to recant the proposition, was so vague as to its meaning that he regarded as valid until its repeal a statute which he expressly declared to violate the *per legem terrae* clause of Magna Carta itself[53]—a clause doubly sacred, under the dictum of Bonham's Case and the repeatedly affirmed immutability of the Great Charter. More representative of Coke's ordinary thought is the phrase which he borrowed from the Year Books: "Parliament is so high and mighty in its Nature, that it may make Laws; and that, that is Law, it may make no Law."[54]

Coke himself in time came to trust the determination of common right and reason in Parliament more readily than in the courts. His own removal from office taught him that the courts, being immediately subject to royal control, could express no independent view on legal questions. Hence he transferred his attention to Parliament, as a body immune from royal interference, and in the House of Commons hoped "that his Tongue may cleave to the Roof of his Mouth, that saith this House is no Court of Record; and he that saith this house hath no Power of Judicature, understands not himself: for, though we have not such Power in all Things, yet we have Power of Judicature in some Things, and therefore it is a Court of Record."[55] Miss Relf has suggested that this new importance of Parliament as the defender of the common law accounts for the revival of jurisdiction by the House of Lords

---

[51] Moore (K.B.) 827-8.
[52] *Ibid.*, 830.
[53] *Second Institute*, 51; *Fourth Institute*, 41.
[54] Parliament, 13 Reports 64.
[55] Nicholas, *op. cit.*, ii, 7.

in 1621, and the increasing attention the Commons gave to private complaints.[56]

But a less partisan observer than Coke might have found little cause for satisfaction in the conduct of judicial business by either house in the 1620's. Nothing more servile than the proceedings against Middlesex occurred in the courts of Westminster Hall; nothing more arbitrary than the Commons' persecution of Floyd occurred in the Star Chamber. There was no warrant either in common law or in statute law for the conviction of Manwaring. In fact, none of the important judicial proceedings in Parliament in that decade, or, at most, only the impeachment of Bacon, was warranted in law and in fact. Little regard was paid either to the question of jurisdiction or to rules of substantive law: "on extraordinary Causes we may enlarge and make Precedents." [57]

One cause for this readiness to play fast and loose with the rules of law was partisan feeling. Apparently another was the common failure to distinguish between the legislative and the judicial functions of Parliament. It was not until the trial of Strafford that a contrast was clearly drawn between making new law and applying the old, and in his argument for the attainder St. John, though he conceded that an attainder was legislation, insisted that Strafford was being attainted for felony, and that attainder was a proper method of punishment. Previous to that time we sometimes find almost an identification of the two functions. In arguing in the House of Commons in 1610 against the decision in Bate's Case, Thomas Hedley insisted: "Also matters in fact and law triable by Parliament. Attaynder of treason in Parliament. No argument that we cannot judge of lawe for that wee be not all lawyers, no more as to say wee cannot passe a bill of clothing for that wee are not all clothiers." [58] To be sure, Sir Robert Hitcham replied, "This judgment *in Scaccario* not alterable

[56] Introduction to *Notes of Debates in the House of Lords, 1621-1628* (Camden Society, ed. Relf).

[57] Sir George Moore on Floyd's Case, Nicholas, *op. cit.*, i, 370.

[58] *Parliamentary Debates in 1610*, p. 72.

in Parliament, except by bill. Not by way of disputacion, etc., as now." But an argument of Coke's indicates that his mind was in the same state as Hedley's: "every one who sitteth here is as a Judge, and hath a Vote negative in the making of the Laws of this Kingdom . . . and therefore none of us are to be examined as Witnesses in any thing whereof this House with the Lords are to be Judges." [59]

It seems, then, that ideas about Parliament were extraordinarily confused, and that its character as a court colored all thinking about it. This makes more intelligible the dictum of Bonham's Case. Coke has been criticized for inconsistency in declaring for judicial review of statutes while on the bench, and for magnifying Parliament when he became a member of the Commons. It seems likely that in both cases he was concerned for something else— for what he conceived to be the common law. After all, he did not say that the King's Bench, or the House of Commons, would control legislation; he said *"the common law* will controul it, and adjudge such act to be void."

A great change is implicit in the actions of the Long Parliament. Parliament is no longer a part of the frame of the common laws; it derives its authority rather from the fact that it is a kind of surrogate for the elements of which the kingdom is composed. Law becomes the creation of Parliament, rather than its creator: it is significant that the only judicial affirmation of the omni-competence of Parliament before the nineteenth century comes in the Commonwealth period.[60] The preconceptions which Coke represents still found expression in the Long Parliament and its apologists, as they find expression today, but they appear only as the standing ruins of what had been in the time of Coke a fairly complete system.

---

[59] Nicholas, *op. cit.,* i, 176. See a similar statement in *The Parliamentary Diary of Robert Bowyer, 1606-1607,* p. 116.

[60] Campbell, *Lives of the Chief Justices* (London, 1874) ii, 56.

Chapter V

THE LEGAL THEORY OF HIGH PREROGATIVE

I. *Forsett's treatment of the prerogative; the extra-national power of the king; the extra-legal power of the king.*

II. *The use of reason of state; Parliamentary repudiation of reason of state; acts of state.*

I

THE philosophical theory of kingship set forth by writers like James and Manwaring was not logically compatible with a legal theory of prerogative. If the king was the source and sanction of law, he should be in all cases, and not merely in the respects specified by the law of prerogative, *solutus legibus*. But English history and English law presented the crown with the prerogative, impossible to disclaim and useful to assert. Consequently royalist theorists sought and achieved a superficial amalgamation of royalist theory and legal principles. Edward Forsett's *Comparative Discourse of the Bodies Natural and Politique*[1] illustrates the manner in which this was done. Forsett develops the familiar theory of monarchy, that the king "doth severally convey and impart to any part of his dominions, the verie essentiall faculties of his government; without the which no people can ever as subjects raunge themselves into the order, and communitie of humane societie, howsoever, as men, or rather as wild savages, they may perhaps breath a while upon the earth." He shows that the sovereign possesses this faculty of inspiring

[1] London, 1606.

order by drawing analogies to the soul, the head, and the heart in man: he chooses these analogies, rather than the more familiar ones of the angels and sheep and bees, because "in the very composure of man, there is manifestly discovered a summary abstract of absolute perfection, by which as by an absolute Idea, or an exact rule, we may examine and exemplifie all other things." Having established, by the nature of man, the necessity that in all organization, and consequently in the body politic, there be a "first wheele & string of motion, giving force and order to the whole frame," he qualifies this theory of irresponsible rule by the prime mover by subjecting him in turn to a principle of order: "In man the soule ruleth by reason, and in the State the Soveraigne governeth by lawes; which may no lesse aptly be termed the soule of soveraignty, than reason is said to be the soule of the soule. . . . So government may not be so much as imagined to be without law, though the force and life of the law, through the waywardnesse of the subjects, cannot alwayes alike be shewed or seene in his due effects: no not the Soveraigne will infringe lawes, no more than the soule will renounce reason."

Nevertheless, there is a prerogative of extraordinary rule: "To this likeness of God and the soule, let us also shape our Soveraigntie: which (besides that which is regular in regiment, from his power and goodnes imparted to the people) hath still, and reteineth to it selfe certaine prerogative rights of most ample extensions, and most free exemptions, whereof true reverence (filled with all submissive acknowledgments, and contented with that portion and interest which it receiveth from regalitie) admitteth no questioning disputes, and whereof just governours do not so farre inlarge the lists, as to do what they lust, but do so moderate the use (as God in the world, and the Soule in the body) not to the impeach, but to the support of justice; not to the hurt, but to the good of subjects."

Thus Forsett reconciles his theory of law with prerogative. He has done nothing toward reconciling his theory of law with the Parliamentary theory of law, or his theory of prerogative with the Parliamentary theory of prerogative. To Forsett, the prerogative was the king's power to emancipate himself from his own laws; to the Parliamentarians, it was the legal provision made by the common law for the king. It is a far cry from Forsett's theory to Selden's acid remark: "Prerogative is something that cann be told what it is, not something that has no name. Just as you see the Arch Bishopp has his prerogative Court, but we knowe what is done in that Court, so the King's prerogative [is] not his will, or what Divines make it, a power to doe what he lists. The Kings Prerogative, that is the Kings Law. For Example, if you aske, if a patron may present to a living after six monthes by Lawe, I answer no, If you aske whether the King may, I answer the King may by his prerogative, that is by the Law, that concernes him in that case." [2]

The lawyers upon whom James and Charles relied to maintain the interests of the crown were on the side of Selden rather than Forsett. They belonged to the jurisprudential rather than the naturalistic school of thought; they derived the powers of the king from law rather than the law from the king. A few lawyers, like Bacon and Ellesmere, were sufficiently attracted by metaphysical speculation to attempt to make philosophy and law run in double harness. But the jurists who between 1600 and 1640 boldly and ably sketched out the theory of high prerogative: Chief Baron Fleming, Sir John Davies, Serjeant Ashley, Sir Robert Heath, Sir Robert Berkeley, and the rest, were merely lawyers who believed that the law vested certain transcendent powers in the king. Prerogative was something that could be told what it was, and they gave it a name.

There were three great constitutional issues in the period 1600-1640: the king's right to levy impositions, decided in Bate's Case

---

[2] *Table Talk*, title Prerogative.

(1606); the king's right to arrest for reason of state without alleging a cause, decided in the Five Knights' Case (1627); the king's right to levy taxes without the consent of Parliament, on the plea of necessity, decided in Hampden's Case (1638). In each of these the crown lawyers won the decision, which is not surprising when one considers that the bench was rather carefully staffed for that purpose. There were two chief arguments employed by the crown in these cases, two features of the prerogative. Both were outlined by Chief Baron Fleming in Bate's Case, but the first was the main reliance in the question of impositions; the second became the stock royalist theory of prerogative after 1620.

Fleming grounded the king's right to levy impositions upon two principles: the king's authority was extra-national, and in international concerns was not limited by the national law; and it was supra-legal, so that he might for reason of state legally act contrary to the common law.

The first ground of decision alone was sufficient for Bate's Case, and upon that Sir John Davies grounded his book, *The Question concerning Impositions*.[3] The king was king outside Britain, and the common law was confined to England; consequently, he could impose duties upon goods entering England without infringing the common law. This power of levying duties was communicated to the king by the law of nations, which described the rights of kings in virtue of sovereignty.

For as the Law of Nations was before Kings, for Kings were made by the Law of Nations, *Ex jure Gentium Reges originem traxerunt,* saith Baldus; So Kings were no sooner made by the Law of Nations, but presently the same Law, *cum creatus fuerit Rex ei omnia regalia conceduntur, & competit omnibus Regibus jus imponendi quantum habet Regalia,* saith Baldus, *Vectigalia introducta sunt a jure, &c.* which is the Law of Nature or Nations, . . . did annex this Prerogative to their several Crowns.

. . . Then came the positive Law, and limited the Law of Nations, whereas

---

[3] The book was written toward the end of the reign of James I, but was not published until 1656.

by the Law of Nations the King had an absolute and unlimited power in all matters whatsoever. By the positive Law the King himself was pleased to limit and stint his absolute power, and to tye himself to the ordinary rules of the Law, in common and ordinary cases, worthily and princely, according to the Roman Emperour, *Dignissimum Principe Rex se allegatum legibus confiteri*, retaining and reserving notwithstanding in many points that absolute and unlimited power which was given unto him by the Law of Nations, and in these cases or points, the Kings Prerogatives do consist.

This historical treatment of the law is strikingly like that of royalist theorists such as James and Hayward; but it is also like that of such a Parliamentarian as Coke. On the critical question of the nature of law, Davies appears to agree with Coke rather than with the royalist theorists. Both the law of nations and the positive law exist apart from the king's will: the king's power is derivative from the law of nations, and save for the prerogative he is bound by the positive law.

According to Davies the absolute prerogative, which inheres in the scepter, cannot be taken away by any act of Parliament. Here reason of state comes in:

this being a Prerogative in point of Government, as well as in point of profit, it cannot be restrained or bound by Act of Parliament, it cannot be limited by any certain or fixt Rule of Law, no more than the course of a Pilot upon the Sea, who must turn the Helme, or bear higher or lower sail according to the wind and weather; and therefore it may properly be said, That the King's Prerogative in this point is as strong as *Samson,* it cannot be bound; for though an Act of Parliament be made to restrain it, and the King doth give his consent unto it, as *Samson* was bound with his own consent, yet if the Philistines come, that is, if any just or important occasion do arise, it cannot hold or restrain the Prerogative, it will be as thred, and broken as easie as the bonds of Samson.

To the first argument, that the king's power was extra-national, it was replied succinctly and forcibly in the House of Commons that "The comon lawe extends as farre [as] the power of the king extends. It is as soule in the body."[4] The Commons were much

---

[4] *Parliamentary Debates in 1610* (Camden Society, ed. Gardiner) p. 89.

longer in formulating a reply to "reason of state." The principle rested upon an obvious political necessity, and had long gone unchallenged.

The term "reason of state" appeared in Italy early in the sixteenth century. It was in Italy that active and sustained international relations first developed, among the ambitious city-states of the Renaissance. An indication of the new order of political life is the permanent maintenance of ambassadors at foreign capitals; several Italian cities were following such a practice by the end of the fifteenth century, and during the following century the northern nations took it up, somewhat irregularly. The wars of religion, the intrigues, the plots of assassination gave an added significance to international affairs, and increased the importance of diplomacy and political concerns. Such matters were "reason of state"; they were of necessity secret, unpredictable, and peremptory.

That such affairs should be left to the discretion of the king, even though he might be compelled to act suddenly without Parliament or in contravention of the ordinary law, seemed so reasonable that at first, at least, Parliamentarians conceded the claim. Elizabeth in 1571 warned her Parliament that "they should do well to meddle with no matters of state, but such as should be propounded unto them," [5] and enforced the decree with considerable success. So good a Parliamentarian as Sir Robert Cotton could say, "I am not ignorant, that this latter age hath brought forth a swarm of busie heads, which measure the great Mysteries of State, by the rule of their self-conceited wisdoms; but if they would consider, that the Commonwealth, governed by grave Counsellors, is like unto a Ship directed by a skillful pilot, whom the necessities of occasions, and grounds of reason, why he steereth to this, or that point of the Compass, are better known, than to those that stand aloof off; they would perhaps be more sparing, if

---

[5] *Hansard's Parliamentary History,* i, 730.

not more wary in their resolutions." [6] In James' second letter of rebuke to the House of Commons in 1621 he insisted "these are unfit Things to be handled in Parliament, except your King should require it of you: for who can have Wisdom to judge of Things of that Nature, but such as are daily acquainted with the Particulars of Treaties, and of the variable or fixed Connexion of Affairs of State, together with the Knowledge of Secret Ways, Ends and Intentions of Princes, in their several Negotiations?" [7] Although he resented this denial of Parliamentary privilege, Sir Robert Phelips counselled, "He would not therefore have us roll this Stone further, seeing it is for Point of State, that his Majesty now spareth to have the Laws against Papists strictly executed." [8] It was not until it became clear that Charles was using the excuse of secrecy and urgency in matters domestic rather than foreign that a man like Richard James could say "the secrett of government, *arcanus imperii,* not to be named: 'tis a word of tyrannie. In faire governments all is cleere and open." [9]

At least in royalist theory, it was not only expedient but lawful that the king exercise his absolute prerogative in matters of state. Bacon said in his *Essay on Judicature:* [10]

Fourthly, for that which may concern the sovereign and estate. Judges ought above all to remember the conclusion of the Roman Twelve Tables; *Salus populi suprema lex;* [the supreme law of all is the weal of the people;] and to know that laws, except they be in order to that end, are but things captious, and oracles not well inspired. Therefore it is an happy thing in a state when kings and states do often consult with judges; and again when judges do often consult with the king and state: the one, when there is matter of law intervenient in business of state; the other, when there is some consideration of state intervenient in matter of law. For many times the things deduced to judgment may be *meum* and *tuum,* when the reason and conse-

---

[6] *Cottoni Posthuma* (1884) ii, 37.
[7] [Nicholas,] *Proceedings and Debates of the House of Commons, 1620-1621* (1766) ii, 323.
[8] *Ibid.,* ii, 334.
[9] Manuscript comment on Eliot's *Monarchie of Man.* Grosart's Introduction to the *Monarchie of Man,* i, 118.
[10] *Works* (ed. Spedding) xii, 269.

quence thereof may trench to point of estate: I call matter of estate, not only the parts of sovereignty, but whatsoever introduceth any great alteration or dangerous precedent; or concerneth manifestly any great portion of people. And let no man weakly conceive that just laws and true policy have any antipathy; for they are like the spirit and sinews, that one moves with the other.

And "quaint old Tom Fuller" said of *The Just Judge,* "He counts, the rules of state and the laws of the realm mutually support each other.—Those who made the laws to be not only desparate, but even opposite terms to maxims of government, were true friends neither to laws nor government. Indeed, *salus reipublicae* is *charta maxima:* extremity makes the next the best remedy." [11]

The division of political affairs implied in this theory of the absolute prerogative was not exclusively royalist. We have seen that Sir John Eliot considered monarchy to consist of the adjudication of *meum* and *tuum* and of "government." Government was the field of public rather than private affairs: it included those actions which escaped any merely legal classification, such as relations with foreign powers, treaties, negotiations, and sudden domestic emergencies—in short, "matter of state." This province of state affairs would necessarily take precedence over merely private concerns, and thus it was that Justice Berkeley said, "There is a rule of law and a rule of government, and many things may be done by the rule of government that may not be done by the rule of law." [12] Sir Edward Coke himself confessed, following Bate's Case, that the king's power was double, disputable and indisputable.[13] It was possible for these lawyers, and for the royalist lawyers, to affirm that the absolute prerogative was a legal power assigned to the king by the law, and that reason of state was a proper and legal vehicle for its exercise. On the other hand, it was impossible for

---

[11] *The Holy State* (1642) Book IV, Chap. VII.

[12] *Articles of Accusation against the Judges* (London, 1641). Berkeley's opinion in *Howell's State Trials,* iii, 1102 is not so clearly stated. See a similar statement by Whitelocke, *Howell's State Trials,* iii, 289.

[13] *Supra,* p. 56.

a royalist theorist of the stamp of Forsett to accept the limitations implicit in the theory of the absolute prerogative. The absolute prerogative is indeed consistent with his ideal of the good sovereign, taking extraordinary measures for the welfare of his subjects; but in his theory the fact that enables him to take these extraordinary measures is not that they are for the welfare of his subjects, but that he is sovereign. Forsett is obliged to confess that his sovereign might abuse his power: "were the Soveraignes uncorrupted with that all-taynting canker of sinne, and free from every human infirmitie, their wille alone were undoubted law and Justice; but on the other side, when reason (whose office is to shew the right) is vanquished by the errours of misconceiving, then the will by such bad direction is driven to sinne in his designed works: So where the judgement of the Soveraigne swarveth from sincerity of true discerning, there his will and all decrees, or executions following the same, must of necessitie be culpable and turne to wrong." These actions of the sovereign will be morally culpable, but they will still be actions of the sovereign. The royalist lawyers, on the other hand, would join the Parliamentarians in condemning such actions as illegal; for the absolute prerogative was given to the king only to be legitimately used for the *salus populi*.

II

The absolute prerogative was therefore reconcilable with the position of the common lawyers in Parliament, and it was some time before the Parliament came to the point of denying it, or, what is the same thing, tying it strictly to the common law rule of precedent. In the debate on impositions in the Parliament of 1610 the term reason of state was bandied about freely, and only Thomas Hedley made a forthright protest: "This question determinable onely by the common lawe of England, for lawe of State he knowes not." [14] Carleton, who likewise opposed the impositions,

---

[14] *Parliamentary Debates in 1610*, p. 72.

argued: "It is not reason of state that must rule it. If it do, you must know that this reason of state is not such a monster as a gentleman (Mr. Yelverton) here hath made it. Reason of state is preservation of the state, and not the ruyne of the state . . . we are so farr from making this matter of imposicions reason of state, that even in the 3d. which is imposed upon the stranger merchant above our owne, when we are questioned about it by strangers, we have no other answer but this, 'Nolumus leges Angliae mutari.' It is therefore in the law of the land where we must seek the truth of this matter." [15] Carleton apparently admitted the force of reason of state in a proper case, but chose to judge of the case himself.

The plea of reason of state was employed in that Parliament to justify impositions; it was used in later Parliaments to defend the right of the king to imprison by special warrant without naming a cause and to hold the prisoner without bail. Sir Edward Coke thought that "a Reason of State is a trick to put a man out of the right way; for, when a man can give no reason for a thing, then he flieth to a higher Strain, and saith it is a Reason of State," [16] but he twice admitted, or rather insisted, in the Parliament of 1621, "that a man committed by the Body of the Privy Council may not be bailed, as hath been resolved by all the Judges of the Kingdom: —that it is inconvenient and may be dangerous to have in a Business of State the Reason expressed in the Mittimus." [17] But Coke's friend Selden was arrested in June, 1621, by a warrant which recited merely that the arrest was "for special Causes and Reasons of State," [18] and Coke himself was sent to the Tower in December. Coke never spoke again in favor of reason of state; and all his party abandoned the dangerous doctrine. In the conferences between the Commons and the Lords on the Petition of Right, the

---

[15] *Ibid.*, p. 110n.

[16] Nicholas, *op. cit.*, i, 308.

[17] *Ibid.*, ii, 25, 209.

[18] The warrant is printed in the appendix of *Proceedings and Debates of the House of Commons, 1620-1621*, ii.

Commons urged that such imprisonment without cause shown was contrary to Magna Carta. Serjeant Ashley, who was attending the Lords, argued that reason of state gave supplementary authority to the king beyond his rights under the common law.[19]

. . . the Question will aptly be made, whether the King or Council may commit to Prison *per Legem Terrae?* And if they may, whether of necessity they must alledge a Cause?

To deliver this, we must consider what is *Lex Terrae,* which is not so strictly to be taken as if *Lex Terrae* were only that Part of the Municipal Law which we calle the Common Law; for there are divers other Jurisdictions exercised in this Kingdom, which are also to be reckoned the Law of the Land. As in *Cawdrey's* Case, in the 5th Report, Fol. 8. The Ecclesiastical Law is held the Law of the Land. . . .

The Admiral Jurisdiction is also *Lex Terrae,* for Things done upon the Sea. . . .

The Martial Law likewise, . . .

And so it is also in the Case of the Law Merchant, . . .

In like Manner it is in the Law of State; when the Necessity of State requires it, they do and may proceed according to Natural Equity, as in those other Cases; because, in Cases where the Law of the Land provides not, there the Proceedings may be by the Law of Natural Equity; and infinite are the Occurrents of State unto which the Common Law extends not; and if this Proceeding of State should not also be accounted the Law of the Land, then do we fall into the same Inconvenience mentioned in *Cawdrye's* Case, that the King should not be able to do Justice in all Cases within His own Dominions.

If then the King or His Council may not commit, it must needs follow, that either the King must have no Council of State, or having such a Council, they must have no Power to make Orders or Acts of State. . . .

I therefore conclude, That, for Offences against the State, in Cases of State Government, the King or His Council hath lawful Power to punish by Imprisonment, without shewing particular Cause, where it may tend to the disclosing of the Secrets of State Government.

Littleton for the Commons made the significant reply that "we read of no Law of State,"[20] and argued that *lex terrae* was the common law.

---

[19] *Lords Journal,* iii, 758.
[20] *Ibid.,* p. 761. For Littleton's reply see *supra,* p. 50.

This eventual repudiation of reason of state was the result of the increasing employment of the principle by king and Council. It first received open acknowledgement in legal theory in Bate's Case. During the second decade of the century it was a cause commonly cited for granting and for cancelling patents of monopoly. Very revelatory is a letter of the Privy Council to the Lord Deputy of Ireland, ordering him to adjudicate a private dispute, taking into consideration "as well matter of State and government of that country, as matter of justice and right, together alsoe with matter of equity and conscience, and accordinge to all these (if the parties shall not otherwise consent in some arbitrary course), finally to order, determyne, and decree the same cause." [21] In 1620, in regard to a claim for a tithe of the lead ore mined in High Peak in the county of Derby, "their Lordships made answere that haveing taken mature consideracion of that cause both for matter of justice and pointe of State" they recommended a suit, "and concerning the point of State, their Lordships have ordered a course to informe themselves whether those works of myne in leade oare will beare this dutie of tithe in such proporcion as is now demanded." [22] After these intrusions of reason of state in the adjudication of *meum* and *tuum,* we are not surprised to find a new kind of legislation bearing the name. Acts of Parliament we know, and proclamations, but now we hear of Acts of State, as in a letter of 1620 where we read that the charter of London has been surrendered and a more moderate one is to be granted, and that to prevent regranting of such excessive privileges as the former charter conferred, "his Majesty was further pleased to command an Act of State to be made and entred in the Register of Councell causes, that if any of the aforesaid particulars contayned in the late surrendered grant, or any flower of his Majesty's crowne or other point either of his honor or prerogative, shall by surreption

---

[21] *Acts of the Privy Council, 1616-1617,* p. 82.
[22] *Acts of the Privy Council, 1619-1621,* p. 317.

or otherwise be procured under his Majesty's hand and so passed the seales, the graunt or grauntes thereof be ymediately *ipso facto* voyd and of noe force." [23] More important of course were the political arrests from 1621 to 1629 for reason of state, and the extortion of taxes under the plea of emergency.

The great problems of state fell into two classes: the management of diplomacy and secret negotiation, and national affairs not secret but urgent. It was with the first category that James I was engrossed: his concern with European politics and his endless negotiations brought him a belief in the transcendent importance of such matters, and he valued the absolute prerogative chiefly as an instrument for enforcing secrecy in "mysteries of state." He was quite sincere in his insistence that the Commons should not tamper with these affairs; his great quarrel with Parliament in 1621 grew out of nothing else than his statesman's fear of meddlers. Charles, on the other hand, was perhaps less than honest in his application of the principle. His arrests in the latter '20's had nothing to do with foreign politics, and the national emergencies upon which he relied in the '30's were more or less fictitious. To be sure, there was every rational ground, as Justice Berkeley said in Hampden's Case, for allowing the king an extraordinary power to meet sudden crises, and there was no practicable alternative to making the king sole judge of the emergency. English law today allows the crown such a power. But the only emergency Charles could truly claim was the need for extraordinary sources of revenue which his incapacity for dealing with Parliaments caused, and this was not properly within the purview of reason of state. It is true that Charles' frauds were not subject to examination and censure in the Exchequer Chamber, and it is therefore difficult to see how the judges could have reached any other decision than

---

[23] *Ibid.*, p. 323. Act of state became a common name for proclamations. Strafford was alleged to have told the Irish that "they must expect lawes as from a conqueror, and an act of state should bee as binding as an act of parliment." Verney, *Notes of Proceedings in the Long Parliament* (Camden Society, ed. Bruce) p. 63.

they did in Hampden's Case. Only by rejecting the philosophy of reason of state could they have found for Hampden. This was the course the Parliamentarians had taken earlier: they had dissociated themselves from the continental doctrine of reason of state and from the theory of sovereignty conferred by the law of nations, and had grounded government firmly on the common law.The royalist lawyers in working out the argument of absolute prerogative were developing a legitimate tradition, but they were furnishing merely a legal apology for a court whose genuine pretensions required no less a vindication than the theory of complete sovereignty set forth by Forsett and Manwaring and Filmer.

CHAPTER VI

ROYALIST THEORIES OF KINGSHIP

TWO separate supports of the theory of kingship were set
forth by the royalist theorists of the time. The first was
what we should call today a theory of sovereignty. It was
the proposition that political organization existed only by virtue
of the command-relationship of superiority on the part of the king
and subjection on the part of the subjects. It differed from our
modern theories of sovereignty in that it was a naturalistic rather
than a jural theory: sovereignty was not a legal right resulting from
legal relations, but a natural fact which gave rise to law and legal
relations. And, as a natural institution which had its counterparts
in all the other natural dominions in the universe—the rule of God,
the rule of the father of the family, the rule of the shepherd over
his flock, the rule of the soul in the body—it was a purposive, pro-
tecting agency, which existed because it had a definite function

to perform. Consequently sovereignty was in the seventeenth century a moral rule, whereas today it is mere will and force.

The second argument was the royalist use of history. Historically, so these theorists asserted, the king had been a natural ruler unlimited by law, who by his own power brought the political community into being. Subsequently he promulgated laws; since they were expressions of his will, he could unmake them. The first argument, the theory of sovereignty, could be employed without the second, as it was by Edward Forsett. The second could be employed without any explicit use of the first, as it was by Sir Peter Hayward; but to arrive at the usual royalist conclusion of an unfettered king it must assume the relation between sovereign and law set forth in the first argument, for unless law derived its strength and being from the will of the sovereign it was of no avail to argue that at one time the king had not been bound by laws. Sir Edward Coke admitted that once the king had not been bound by law; but to Coke law had an existence independent of the will of the sovereign, and now that it had come into being it limited the power of the crown. The high prerogative lawyers, too, agreed with Coke that a certain sphere of law existed which maintained itself without the help of the sovereign: they differed from Coke in arguing that the crown possessed reserved power to act outside the law in particular fields. The royalist philosophers went beyond this, and placed the sovereignty of the king above all law.

These two arguments are common to most of the royalist publicists of the period; the conspicuous exception is Hobbes. The three great systematists of the royalist cause were King James, Roger Manwaring, and Sir Robert Filmer. It may be instructive to examine in detail the theories of each, not merely to observe the use of history and of the theory of sovereignty, but also to note the variations introduced by the individual theorists. And Charles I deserves mention because of his historical importance, even though he was no philosopher.

I

The greater part of James' political writing was a direct result of the Gunpowder Plot. His *Apologie,* his *Premonition,* and his *Defence* are all directed at the writers, particularly Bellarmine, who argued that it was lawful for the pope to depose kings, or for subjects to kill heretical or tyrannical rulers. He is particularly incensed at the doctrine of tyrannicide, and one of his chief arguments against deposition is that it is likely to lead to the death of the king. It is apparent that his feelings are aroused: "O hel-hounds, O diabolical wretches, O infernall monsters!" thus he salutes the advocates of rebellion.

The argument in these works follows the course familiar since the middle ages. The Church possesses the power of excommunication, but this can carry no temporal force, and subjects are in no way released from their obligation to a heretical or excommunicated ruler.[1] The Bible clearly enjoins subjects to submit even to persecutors of the Christian faith, and the example of the fathers of the Church further demonstrates this duty. The alleged power of the pope to depose is usurped, and goes contrary to Scripture and the best examples of former times. In fact, the papacy is itself Antichrist, and can claim no Christian authority of any kind.

Not merely is there a deficiency of power in the Church to intervene in temporal affairs; it is also true that there is a supreme jurisdiction placed in kings by God himself. Kings are deputies of God, his lieutenants; they sit on his throne and wield his scepter. Just what this means it is hard to say. Does it mean that royal power is literally divine, and inferentially unlimited? James seems to use the argument in a more moderate manner. He employs it to controvert the papal claim of a right to depose, and the Jesuit doctrine of tyrannicide. He uses it also to discourage secular rebellion; here it seems equivalent to the doctrine of passive obedience. He uses it to characterize the rule of a lawful king as part of the moral order

---

[1] *Political Works of James I* (ed. McIlwain) pp. 113, 205, 212, 232.

of the universe, in the same manner as Hooker. These are limits on the rights of pope and subject, rather than descriptions of the power of the king. If one takes at face value James' claim of viceregency, his is throughout a theological system, a version of the doctrine of the two swords. But there is reason to believe that when he came to put an active content into royal power James turned to quite another source. His argument from Scripture was primarily a defensive argument, intended to dissuade potential assassins. His theory of sovereignty was in terms of a native, underived power in the king, which he possessed immediately in his own right rather than as a deputy of God. James describes the power of the king in Aristotelian terms; he confines the spiritual power—the papacy, and subjects acting against the king on a religious pretext—by theological arguments.

James has no very clear idea of the place of the Church in the state. Apparently it is distinct from the king, for it can excommunicate him. It has the duty to advance the cause of God by teaching and the use of spiritual censures, even in despite of the king.[2] But everything material—the corporal punishment of heresy, for example—belongs to the king.[3] The king as a Christian is bound to promote the true faith, but his authority does not depend upon his orthodoxy. His Christian subjects can contest misrule only with tears and prayers.

James once refers to a general Council as a means of settling questions of faith, but has little hope of the outcome.[4] Undoubtedly he felt that his own actions should be governed by his own opinions rather than those of any assembly of churchmen. His opinions were latitudinarian; he was willing to tolerate tender consciences, but complete apostates he would burn.[5]

---

[2] *Ibid.*, p. 213.

[3] *Ibid.*, p. 232.

[4] *Ibid.*, pp. 151, 207.

[5] Two heretics were burned in 1612, on writs *de heretico comburendo*. Stephen, *History of the Criminal Law of England*, ii, 462.

It is a great pity that he never read Marsiglio, for his system could easily be stiffened into consistency in the direction of Marsiglio's teaching. He declares that priests are in no way exempt from their allegiance to the king, but he does not discuss, as Marsiglio does, the spiritual character of priesthood.

Nor is there any clear indication of James' ideas as to the relation of the supernatural to the natural universe. God's injunction that Christian subjects should obey their kings adds a supernatural obligation to a natural obligation, and, so to speak, supernaturalizes the natural. On the other hand, in his discussion of episcopacy James naturalizes the supernatural. Episcopacy, he says, is ordained by God; furthermore, a law of nature requires the institution.[6]

That Bishops ought to be in the Church, I ever maintained it, as an Apostolique institution, and so the ordinance of God; contrary to the *Puritanes,* and likewise to *Bellarmine;* who denies that Bishops have their Jurisdiction immediately from God (But it is no wonder that he takes the *Puritanes* part, since *Jesuits* are nothing but *Puritan-papists*). And as I ever maintained the state of Bishops, and the Ecclesiasticall Hierarchie for order sake; so was I ever an enemie to the confused Anarchie or paritie of the *Puritanes,* as well appeareth in my *Basilikon Doron.* Heaven is governed by order, and all the good Angels there; nay, Hell it selfe could not subsist without some order; And the very devils are divided into Legions, and have their chiefetaines: how can any societie then upon earth, subsist without order and degrees?

It would be supplying James with a rationalization which he never made for himself to say that this relation of superiority and inferiority, command and obedience, constituted the natural principle of the universe, and that God's rôle was to add divine authority to the established system—to supernaturalize the natural. But at any rate this seems to be James' view of kingship, if not of the entire universe. The only "state of nature" he will recognize is kingship; without a sovereign, men are a headless multitude.

---

[6] *Political Works,* p. 126.

To the natural obligation of subjects is added the supernatural obligation of Christians.

The naturalism of King James has been too much slighted. As prominent as references to divine authority in his writings are expressions like "natural king," "natural allegiance," "natural obligation," "natural duty." The relation of king and subjects is a natural, direct, and primary one, comparable to that of the patriarch and his family.[7] The fatherhood of God, the fatherhood of the king, the fatherhood of the patriarch, are all examples of a principle of natural sovereignty—a principle obtaining even in hell, as we have seen.

And the agreement of the Law of nature in this our ground with the Lawes and constitutions of God, and man, already alledged, will by two similitudes easily appeare. The King towards his people is rightly compared to a father of children, and to a head of a body composed of divers members: For as fathers, the good Princes, and Magistrates of the people of God acknowledged themselves to their subjects. And for all other well ruled Common-wealths, the stile of *Pater patriae* was ever, and is commonly used to Kings. And the proper office of a King towards his Subjects, agrees very wel with the office of the head towards the body, and all members thereof: For from the head, being the seate of Judgement, proceedeth the care and foresight of guiding, and preventing all evill that may come to the body or any part thereof. The head cares for the body, so doeth the King for his people. As the discourse and direction flowes from the head, and the execution according thereunto belongs to the rest of the members, every one according to their office: so it is betwixt a wise Prince, and his people. As the judgement comming from the head may not onely imploy the members, every one in their owne office, as long as they are able for it; but likewise in case any of them be affected with any infirmitie must care and provide for their remedy, in-case it be curable, and if otherwise, gar cut them off for feare of infecting of the rest: even so is it betwixt the Prince, and his people. [8]

---

[7] "There bee three principall similitudes that illustrates the state of MONARCHIE: one taken out of the word of GOD; and the two other out of the grounds of Policie and Philosophie. In the Scriptures Kings are called Gods, and so their power after a certaine relation compared to the Divine power. Kings are also compared to Fathers of Families: for a King is trewly *Parens patriae*, the politique father of his people. And lastly, Kings are compared to the head of this Microcosme of the body of man." *Political Works*, p. 307.

[8] *Ibid.*, p. 64.

So thoroughly does James assimilate the authority of the king to that of the father that he affirms regicides to be parricides, and demonstrates the unnaturalness of rebellion by showing that in all nature only the vipers turn upon their parents.[9] But the power of a father is no complete measure of the power of kings, for kings are of greater dignity: in the hierarchy of authorities in which the universe is ranged, they stand next to God, and are called by God (apparently in an analogical sense) Gods on earth.

The kingdom derives from the king, for without him there would be anarchy. Consequently King James believed that his accession to the throne of England had joined England and Scotland into the Kingdom of Great Britain. Law is the force by which the king holds society together. The king is not confined by law, for he is "both the author and giver of strength thereto." Nevertheless,

A good king will not onely delight to rule his subjects by the lawe, but even will conforme himselfe in his own actions thereuneto, alwaies keeping that ground, that the health of the common-wealth be his chiefe lawe: And when he sees the lawe doubtsome or rigorous, hee may interpret or mitigate the same, lest otherwise *Summum ius* bee *summa injuria:* And therefore generall lawes, made publikely in Parliament, may upon knowen respects to the King by his authoritie bee mitigated, and suspended upon causes onely knowen to him. [10]

This demonstrates the superiority of the king to the law, but it also demonstrates the purposive character of sovereign power. The true nature of power was to protect and guide, rather than to work injustice. The king might use his power in a manner culpable in a moral sense: this was still an exercise of regal power, not to be contested by subjects, but it was a misuse of power.

For I doe acknowledge, that the speciall and greatest point of difference that is betwixt a rightfull King and an usurping Tyrant is in this: That whereas the proude and ambitious Tyrant doeth thinke his Kingdome and people are onely ordeined for satisfaction of his desires and unreasonable appetites; The righteous and just King doeth by the contrary acknowledge

---

[9] *Ibid.*, p. 65.
[10] *Ibid.*, p. 63.

himselfe to be ordeined for the procuring of the wealth and prosperitie of his people, and that his greatest and principall worldly felicitie must consist in their prosperitie.[11]

James of course thought himself a good king, and was bound to consider factious and self-interested any attempt to resist the genuine national interest for which he stood.

But for himself, he would never make a Separation of the People's Will, and the Will of the King; and as for them that would make any Scissure or Rupture, either of the Church, or of the Commonwealth, and therein were such Schismaticks, he ever esteemed Schismaticks and Hereticks subject to the same Curse. [12]

So much for James' philosophy of kingship. He employed as well a very elaborate historical argument which arrived at the same conclusions. Philosophically, law derived from the King; historically it was his creation. James summarized the history of Scotland thus:

For as our Chronicles beare witnesse, this Ile, and especially our part of it, being scantly inhabited, . . . there comes our first King Fergus, with a great number with him, out of Ireland, which was long inhabited before us, and making himself master of the countrey, by his own friendship, and force, as well of the Ireland men that came with him, as of the countreymen that willingly fell to him, he made himselfe King and Lord, as well of the whole lande, as of the whole inhabitants within the same. Thereafter he and his successours, a long while after their being Kinges, made and established their lawes from time to time, and as the occasion required. So the trewth is directly contrarie in our state to the false affirmation of such seditious writers, as would persuade us, that the Lawes and state of our countrey were established before the admitting of a king: where by the countrarie ye see it plainely prooved, that a wise king comming in among barbares, first established the estate and form of government, and therefore made lawes by himselfe, and his successours according thereunto.

The kings therefore in Scotland were before any estates and rankes of men within the same, before any Parliaments were holden, or lawes made: and by them was the land distributed (which at the first was whole theirs) states erected and decerned, and forms of governement devised and established: And so it followes of necessitie, that the kings were the authors and makers of Lawes, and not the Lawes of the kings. . . .

[11] *Ibid.*, p. 278.
[12] *Commons Journal*, i, 314.

. . . And although divers changes have been in other countries of blood Royall, and kingly house, the kingdome being reft by conquest from one another, as in our neighbour countrey in *England,* (which was never in ours) yet the same ground of the kings right over all the land and subjects thereof remaineth alike in all other free Monarchies, as well as in this: For when the Bastard of *Normandie* came into *England,* and made himselfe king, was it not by force, and with a mighty army? Where he gave the Law, and tooke none, changed the Lawes, inverted the order of government. . . . [13]

Since law was the king's will, and the king's will was law, any rule of law might be revoked by a later act of will. So James might assert the original claim of Fergus to the land of the kingdom:

So as if wrong might bee admitted in play (albeit I grant wrong should be wrong in all persons) the King might have a better colour for his pleasure, without further reason, to take the land from his lieges, as overlord of the whole, and doe with it as it pleaseth him, since all that they hold is of him, then, as foolish writers say, the people might unmake the king, and put an other in his roome: But either of them as unlawful, and against the ordinance of God, ought to be alike odious to thought, much lesse put in practice. [14]

In what sense would the king's resumption of the land of the kingdom be "unlawful"? Apparently James' ordinary constitutional ideas differ from his political theory. As sovereign he has complete power, but the exercise of this power may be constitutionally unlawful. This appears paradoxical, and James never resolved the paradox. But there is little danger of misinterpreting him if we gather from his works, and particularly from the speech to the Parliament of 1610,[15] an explanation like this. Among the laws which the king has made are rules for his own future conduct. These are something more than declarations of intention; by long-continued observance they have become the custom of the realm, and have attained a measure of objectivity, a certain independence of the king. The sovereign power can of course override them, but

[13] *Political Works,* pp. 61-2.
[14] *Ibid.,* p. 62.
[15] *Ibid.,* p. 306, especially p. 309. See also James' very moderate attitude toward Parliamentary privilege as reported by Yelverton in 1609. *Archaeologia,* xv.

this is no ordinary repealer: there is genuine collision between the repealer and the custom. The good king will protect these laws, and will not exert his supra-legal power of repealing them; he has in fact at his coronation made an engagement with God to observe such customs of the realm.

Important among the objectified laws by which the king has consented to abide are the "fundamental laws." James told the House of Commons, when it was debating the Act of Union in 1607, that Scotland had no fundamental laws, save the Ius Regis: "those Lawes whereby confusion is avoyded, and their Kings descent mainteined, and the heritage of the succession and Monarchie, which hath bene a Kingdome, to which I am in descent, three hundreth yeeres before Christ." [16] In England, on the other hand, the common law was fundamental, and James always avowed his desire to respect it. The Scottish Parliament could consider and pass only those bills which the king submitted to it, and even then his final approval was the operative force in putting them into effect. James' English predecessors—unwisely, James must have felt—had allowed their Parliaments greater privileges, and those privileges James was in law and in honor bound to maintain.

James appears, then, to have believed that royal legislation had established constitutions for the various kingdoms, and that kings should abide by these constitutions. He was in general well satisfied with the fundamental laws of England: "as a King I have least cause of any man to dislike the Common Law: For no Law can bee more favorable and advantagious for a King, and extendeth further his Prerogative, than it doeth: And for a King of England to despise the Common Law, it is to neglect his owne Crowne." [17]

In all his practical affairs James was content to rest on his prerogative, and to abide by the common law of England. His working

---

[16] *Political Works,* p. 300.

[17] *Ibid.,* p. 310. To be sure, he insisted upon construing the common law: "Precedents in times of Minors, of Tyrants, of Women, of simple Kings, not to be credited." *Commons Journal,* i, 158.

beliefs coincided perfectly with those of high prerogative law-yers:[18] he differed only in claiming for himself a theoretical right which he pledged himself never to exercise outside the constitu-tional system, complete sovereign power. He claimed that right in order to teach subjects their duty, to combat Jesuitical and "popular" errors, rather than because he wished to exercise it. He never did undertake any action for which there was not fairly good legal warrant; he was certainly a more moderate and "con-stitutional" monarch than Henry VII, Henry VIII, or Elizabeth. He came into difficulties with his Parliaments because there was a new spirit in Parliament, rather than in the crown, and particu-larly because the increasing expenses of government raised prob-lems which the Tudors never faced. It is moreover probably true that a re-examination of the reign of James would disclose far less apprehension on the part of subjects, far less jealousy of the crown, than the Whigs have taught us to believe. It would be dif-ficult to find another character who has been so systematically mis-represented and abused by historians as James I by the Whigs. There was in James good will, moderation, and a sincere devotion to the national interest. His system represents an attempt at a monistic state devoted to a general good, like Rousseau's; it has been disparaged by the beneficiaries of the special interests which contested it. If Louis XIV is a fair example of the working of James' theory, then the rotten borough system must be accepted as the necessary outcome of the Parliamentary argument.

II

Roger Manwaring's principles were set forth in *Religion and Allegiance: Two Sermons Preached before the King's Majesty,* on July 4 and July 29, 1627.[19] The purpose of these sermons was to induce the subjects to pay willingly the loans which the King was

---

[18] See *supra,* pp. 56, 81.
[19] The pamphlet was reprinted in London in 1710.

requesting, and the court thought so highly of their persuasive effect that they were printed and widely distributed. For his utterances Manwaring was examined before the House of Lords and adjudged incapable of holding ecclesiastical office in the future, and the book was condemned to be burned. It was outlawed by proclamation in 1628. Charles, however, pardoned Manwaring and preferred him to a series of posts culminating in the bishopric of St. David's.

The work is so rare that it seems best to illustrate Manwaring's theory with copious quotations from *Religion and Allegiance*. The argument in both sermons follows the same course, but the first is somewhat fuller, and for that reason supplies these excerpts.

Manwaring begins with a cosmology, in which James' system of independent natural relations is unified by the rule of a single Commander.

> Unity is the foundation of all difference *and Distinction; Distinction* the mother of *Multitude; Multitude* and number inferre *Relation;* which is the knot and confederation of things different, by reason of some Respect they beare unto each other. These *Relations* and Respects challenge Duties correspondent; according as they stand in distance or neerenesse, afarre off, or neere conjoyn'd.

> Of all Relations, the first and most originall is that between the *Creator,* and the *Creature;* whereby that which is made depends upon the maker thereof, both in *Constitution,* and *Preservation:* for which, that *Creature* doth ever owe to the *Creator,* the actuall & perpetuall performance of that, which, to yts *nature* is most agreeable: which duty is called *Naturall.* And sometimes also is the *Creature* bound to submit in those things, that are quite and cleane against the naturall, both inclination, and constitution thereof; if the Creators pleasure be so to command it: which dutifull submission is called by the Divines, an *Obedientiall capacity,* in that which is made, by all meanes to doe homage to him that made it of meere nothing.

> The next, is that betweene *Husband* and *Spouse;* a respect, which even *Ethnick Antiquity* call'd and accounted *Sacred.* . . .

> Upon this, followed *that* third *bond* of reference which is betweene *Parents,* and *Children.* . . .

> In the fourth place, did likewise accrew that necessary dependance of the *Servant* on his *Lord.* . . .

From all which forenam'd Respects, there did arise that most *high, sacred,* and *transcendent Relation,* which naturally growes betweene *The Lords Anointed,* and their loyall *Subiects:* to, and over whom, their lawfull *Soveraignes* are no lesse then *Fathers, Lords, Kings,* and *Gods* on earth.

. . . as of *One* there arose *many,* so, by this means, doe *Multitudes* become to bee made *One* againe. Which happy *Re-union, Nature* doth by all meanes much affect: but the effecting thereof is the maine and most gratious worke of Religion. Which the wisedome of *Salomon* well seeing, and the *Spirit* that was in him well searching into, hee sends forth the sententious dictates of his divine and Royall wisedome, fenced with no lesse reason, then the fortresse of Religion; in these words following: *I counsell thee, to keepe the Kings commandement, and that in regard of the oath of God.*

According to this argument all relations, all bonds are parts of a single system pyramided up to God. A king therefore exercises a derivative authority: his power is conferred upon him by God.

Now, all things that worke, and have any operation, must (of necessity) worke by some *Power,* or ability which is in them. All *Power* is either such as is *Created,* or *derived* from some higher Cause, or such, as is *Uncreated,* and *Independent.* Of this last kinde, is that *Power* which is in God alone; who is selfe-able in al things, and most puissant of himself, and from, and by no other. All *Powers* created are of God; *no power, unlesse it bee given from above: And all powers,* that are of this sort, *are ordained of God.* Among all the Powers that be ordained of God, the *Regall* is the most high, strong, and large: *Kings* above all, inferiour to none, to no *multitudes* of men, to no *Angell,* to no order of *Angells.* . . . Their *Power* then the highest. No *Power,* in the world, or in the *Hierarchy* of the *Church,* can lay restraint upon these *supreames;* therfore theirs is the *strongest.*

That Sublime Power therefore which resides in earthly *Potentates,* is not a *Derivation,* or *Collection* of humane power scattered among many, and gathered into one head; but a *participation* of Gods owne *Omnipotency,* which hee never did communicate to any *multitudes* of men in the world, but, *onely,* and *immediately,* to his own Vicegerents. And that is his meaning when he saith, *By me Kings raigne; Kings* they are, by my immediate constitution; and by *me* also, doe they Rule, and exercise their so high and large Authority.

It follows that law is the will of the king, and that the rights of subjects have no other source. "The *Lawes,* which make provision for their [the subjects'] reliefe, take their binding force from the *Supreame* will of their *Liege-Lord*."

We should perhaps have noticed earlier that the power of the king, though communicated by God to the king, is named natural as well as divine. The argument appears to be that God has established monarchy, as other relations in the universe, and this is the natural form of organization; it is, however, divine as well, for God has made kings direct partakers in his authority. It follows that subjects have a twofold duty of obedience. As natural beings, or natural phenomena, so to speak, they owe a natural duty to their king, toward whom they occupy a relation comparable to that of of Aristotle's *natura servus* to his master; they are also obliged, as moral beings, to obey the divinity in the king and the divine injunctions to obedience. These are the "natural" and "obediential" capacities to which Manwaring has already referred. The physical universe displays the natural capacity when it follows its own nature, according to the will of God, "the *Heavens*, in moving; the *Earth*, in standing *still*; the *Fire*, in burning, the *Ayre*, and *Water*, in refreshing, cooling, and flowing." It displays the obediential capacity when it acts contrary to its nature in yielding to a miracle, at the will of God. Man likewise has these two manners of conduct.

All the *Obedience* therefore, that Man can challenge from man, is, in part, *Naturall*: as agreeable and convenient to their inclinations: and, in part, *Morall*, in as much as it is *Free* and *Willing*. And this, of right, may every *Superiour* exact of his *Inferiour*, as a due debt: And every *Inferiour* must yeeld it unto his lawfull *Superiour*, for the same reason. *Children*, to *Parents*, in discipline, and Domesticalls: *Servants*, to their *Lords*, in their respective and obliged duties: *Souldiers*, to their *Commanders*, in Martiall affaires. . . : *People* to their *Pastours*, in Conscientious-duties and matters of Salvation: *Subjects*, to their lawfull *Soveraignes*, in the high Concernements, of State and Policie. And this is that *Obedience*, wherewith we are all charged in this Text, by the *Word* of *God*, and *Wisedome* of *Salomon*.

Manwaring describes the duty of obedience in the usual terms. In Manwaring's scheme politics and theology are so intertwined that it seems profitless to inquire with which we are dealing here.

Nay, though any *King* in the world should command flatly against the Law of God, yet were his *Power* no otherwise at all, to be resisted, but, for the not doing of *His will,* in that which is cleerely unlawfull, to indure with patience, whatsoever penalty *His pleasure* should inflict upon them, who in this would desire rather to obey God then Man. By which patient and meeke suffering of their Soveraignes pleasure, they should become glorious *Martyrs:* whereas, by resisting of *His will,* they should forever endure the paine, and staine of odious Traitors, and impious Malefactors.

But, on the other side; if any King shall command that, which stands not in any opposition to the originall Lawes of *God, Nature, Nations,* and the *Gospell;* (though it be not correspondent in every circumstance, to Lawes Nationall, and Municipall) no Subject may, without hazard of his own Damnation, in rebelling against God, *question,* or *disobey* the will and pleasure of his *Soveraigne.*

Manwaring relies almost exclusively upon his theory of divinely conferred sovereignty. He uses the historical argument only to refute the claims of the Parliamentarians. Since power is from God, Adam was the first king. But this is not an argument that modern kings inherit their power from Adam, a thesis which, as Locke showed, is difficult to maintain. It is merely the usual argument that there were kings before there were Parliaments, and that Parliaments derived from the will of the king:

though such *Assemblies,* as are the *Highest,* and greatest *Representations* of a Kingdome, be most *Sacred* and *honourable,* and *necessary* also for those ends to which they were at first instituted, yet know we must, that, ordained they were not to this end, to contribute any *Right* to *Kings,* whereby to challenge *Tributary aydes* and *Subsidiary* helpes; but for the more equall *Imposing,* and more easie *Exacting* of that, which, unto *Kings* doth appertaine, by *Naturall* and *Originall Law,* and *Justice;* as their proper *Inheritance* annexed to their *Imperiall Crownes,* from their very births.

At the conclusion of the first sermon, however, Manwaring takes up specifically the problem of the loan, and argues that it is just and necessary as well as legal.

And therefore, if, by a *Magistrate,* that is Supreame; if upon *Necessity,* extreame and urgent; such Subsidiary helpes be required: a Proportion being held respectively to the abilities of the Persons charged, and the *Summe,* or Quantity, so required, surmount not (too remarkeably) the use and charge for which it was levied; very hard would it be for any man in the world, that should not accordingly satisfie such demaunde; to defend his Conscience, from that heavie prejudice of *resisting the Ordinance of God,* and *receiving* to himselfe *Damnation:* though every of those Circumstances be not observed, which by the Municipall Lawes is required.

Secondly, if they would consider the *Importunities,* that often may be; the urgent and pressing *Necessities* of State, that cannot stay (without certaine and apparent danger) for the *Motion,* and *Revolution* of so great and vast a body, as such Assemblies are; nor yet abide those long and pawsing Deliberations, when they are assembled; nor stand upon the answering of those jealous and *overwary* cautions, and objections made by some, who (wedded over-much to the love of Epidemical and Popular errours) are bent to crosse the Just and lawfull designes of their wise and gratious Soveraignes: and that, under the plausible shewes of singular liberty, and freedom; which, if their Consciences might speake, would appeare nothing more than the satisfying either of private humours, passions, or purposes.

This is a disappointing retreat from the general position of the *Sermons.* These arguments have little relevancy to the question of right; and the concession that the king's action might violate the municipal laws is in direct conflict with the proposition that law is the will of the king. Like James, Manwaring seems to recognize a sort of qualified objectivity in the fundamental laws; they are not repealed, but overridden by the king's higher will. Manwaring probably thought the less of the issue because he neither knew nor cared anything about law. Sufficient to him was the word of God.

III

Filmer's theory of monarchy differs from that of Hobbes only in the device by which he installs his monarch. Whereas Hobbes followed the Parliamentarians of the Civil War period in treating government as an artificial institution established by contract, Filmer employed the traditional royalist conception of kingship as a natural institution which had historically given birth to political society. Filmer's theory of sovereignty, however, is at all points identical with that of Hobbes.[20]

Locke's *First Treatise* has made the historical aspect of Filmer's theory the most familiar. The historical argument is indeed very prominent in Filmer. As is well known, Filmer assimilates political rule to patriarchal authority.

Even the power which God himself exerciseth over Mankind is by Right of Fatherhood; he is both the King and Father of us all; as God hath exalted the Dignity of Earthly Kings, by communicating to them his own Title, by saying *they are gods;* so on the other side he has been pleased as it were to humble himself, by assuming the Title of a King to express his Power, and not the Title of any popular Government.[21]

If we compare the Natural Rights of a Father with those of a King, we find them all one, without any difference at all but only in the Latitude or Extent of them . . . all the Duties of a King are summed up in an Universal Fatherly Care of his People.[22]

God originally conferred upon Adam paternal authority, which is the same thing as political authority: "I see no reason, but that we may call Adam's Family a Commonwealth, except we will wrangle about Words."[23] This authority is solid, objective right, governed by the law of property.[24] Consequently a usurper can seize and possess it; in this manner Nimrod founded the first empire. "Such a qualified Right is found at first in all Usurpers, as is in Thieves who have stolen Goods, and during the time they are possessed of them, have a Title in Law against all others but the

---

[20] "With no small content I read Mr. Hob's Book *De Cive,* and his *Leviathan,* about the Rights of Sovereignty, which no man, that I know, hath so amply and judiciously handled: I consent with him about the Rights of *exercising* Government, but cannot agree to his means of *acquiring* it." *Observations concerning the Original of Government* (in the collection of 1696).

[21] *Directions for Obedience to Government in Dangerous or Doubtful Times* (1696) p. 159.

[22] *Patriarcha* (1680) p. 23.

[23] *Ibid.,* p. 33.

[24] ". . . this Fatherly Empire, as it was of itself hereditary, so it was *alienable* by Patent, and *seizable* by an Usurper, as other goods are: and thus every King that now is, hath a Paternal Empire, either by Inheritance, or by Translation, or Usurpation; so a Father and a King may be all one." *Observations concerning the Original of Government,* p. 190.

true Owners, and such Usurpers to divers intents and Purposes may be obeyed." [25] The usurper never acquires a perfect right; prescription operates only by positive law, and "Divine Right never dies, nor can be lost, or taken away." [26] A usurper should be obeyed in matters conducing to the safety of the subject, which may be taken to be the wish of the proper ruler, but he should never be obeyed in anything aiming at the person of the true governor. But these questions are academic, for a ruler is to be esteemed a lawful ruler, and not a usurper, as one's reputed father is to be accepted.

Like real property, political power follows the rule of primogeniture; and it also follows the law of escheat. If the heir is not known, power reverts to the fathers of the families.[27]

No, the Kingly Power [is not devolved on the multitude; it] escheats in such cases to the Princes and independent Heads of Families: for every Kingdom is resolved into those parts whereof at first it was made. . . . All such prime Heads and Fathers have power to consent in the uniting or conferring of their Fatherly Right of Sovereign Authority on whom they please: And he that is so Elected, claims not his Power as a Donative from the People, but as being substituted properly by God, from whom he receives his *Royal Charter* of an *Universal* Father, though testified by the Ministry of the Heads of the People.

Filmer uses the common argument to show that law historically derived from the king.

. . . a Proof unanswerable, for the superiority of Princes above Laws, is this, That there were Kings long before there were any Laws: For a long time the Word of a King was the only Law; and if Practice (as saith Sir *Walter Raleigh*) declare the Greatness of Authority, even the best Kings of *Judah* and *Israel* were not tied to any Law; but they did whatsoever they pleased in the greatest Matters.[28]

There want not those who Believe, that the first Invention of Laws was to bridle and moderate the over-great Power of Kings; but the truth is, the Original of Laws was for the keeping of the Multitude in order: Popular

[25] *Directions for Obedience,* p. 161.
[26] *Ibid.,* p. 154.
[27] *Patriarcha,* p. 21.
[28] *Ibid.,* p. 79.

Estates could not subsist at all without Laws, whereas Kingdoms were Govern'd many Ages without them.[29]

Custom at first became Lawful only by some Superiour, which did Command or Consent unto their beginning. And the first Power which we find (as it is confessed by all men) is the Kingly Power, which was both in this and all other Nations of the World, long before any Laws, or any other kind of Government was thought of, from whence we must necessarily infer, that the Common Law it self, or Common Customs of this Land, were Originally the Laws and Commands of Kings at first unwritten.[30]

This completes Filmer's argument from history. Except for the insistence upon the divine origin of paternal and political rule, and the heavy reliance upon the English law of property, this is the historical argument found in Hayward and James. It is a nice question how much reliance Filmer placed upon his argument from history. Probably he never consciously dissociated his historical theory from his theory of sovereignty; but it is arguable that the truly constructive part of his system is the theory of sovereignty, and that his historical argument was intended less as a support of his own theory than as a criticism of the rival theory, so prominent in the 1640's, of the creation of the state by contract. Filmer insists that the idea of free and equal individuals in a state of nature is unhistorical; the Old Testament conclusively disproves the theory. He sets up his alternative reading of history primarily in order to refute the contract notion.

I cannot understand how this *Right of Nature* can be conceived without imagining a Company of men at the very first to have been all Created together without any Dependency one of another, or as *Mushrooms (fungore more) they all on a sudden were sprung out of the Earth without any Obligation one to another* as Mr. Hob's words are in his Book *De Cive, cap. 8 sect. 3.* the Scripture teacheth us otherwise, that all men came by Successions, and Generation from one man: We must not deny the Truth of the History of the Creation.[31]

A principal Ground of these Diversities and Contrarieties of Divisions, was

---

[29] *Ibid.,* p. 91.
[30] *Ibid.,* p. 102.
[31] *Observations concerning the Original of Government,* p. 166.

an Error which the Heathens taught, that *all things at first were common,
and that all men were equal.* This mistake was not so heinous in those
Ethnick Authors of the Civil Laws, who wanting the Guide of the History of
Moses, were fain to follow Poets and Fables for their Leaders. But for
Christians, who have read the Scriptures, to dream either of a *community of
all things,* or an *Equality of all Persons,* is a Fault scarce pardonable.[32]

The Biblical account of the donation to Adam was very useful
in refuting the contract theory. It also contributed to Filmer's
theory of sovereignty, and Filmer availed himself liberally of that
support. Yet it is probable that Filmer's theory of sovereignty
requires much less than the complete truth of Filmer's history. The
royalist theory of history in general contributed only the proposition that society came into existence by virtue of the command of
a monarch, and this simple assertion is as adequate for Filmer as
for other writers. It is by no means so conclusive as the patriarchal
theory, but it does provide a historical basis for monarchy.

Filmer's theory of the sovereignty of the monarch is derived
from the proposition that law is the will of a superior: "we all
know that a Law in General is the command of a Superior
Power."[33] This will is necessarily unlimited and arbitrary.

. . . . it is not Power except it be arbitrary: a legislative Power cannot be without being absolved from humane Laws.[34]

We do but flatter our selves, if we hope ever to be governed without an
Arbitrary Power. . . . There never was, nor ever can be any People governed
without a Power of making Laws, and every Power of making Laws must
be Arbitrary: For to make a Law according to Law, is *Contradictio in
adjecto.*[35]

Those who argue that the state is the creation of law have mis-
taken the nature of law.

It is not the Law that is the Minister of God, or that carries the Sword, but
the Ruler or Magistrate; so they that say the Law governs the Kingdom,

[32] *Ibid.,* p. 200.
[33] *Patriarcha,* p. 101.
[34] *Observations concerning the Original of Government,* p. 187.
[35] *Observations concerning the Original of Government: Observations upon Mr. Hunton's
Treatise of Monarchy,* Preface.

may as well say that the Carpenters Rule builds an House, and not the Carpenter; for the Law is but the Rule or Instrument of the Ruler.[36]

Law is will, but it is not a dead edict; to Filmer law is the continuous will of the commander who puts it into execution.

No man can say, that during the Reign of Queen *Elizabeth,* that King *Henry* the Eighth, or *Edward* the Sixth did govern, although that many of the Laws that were made in those two former Princes times, were observed, and executed under her Government; who willed and commanded the Execution of them, and had the same Power to correct, interpret, and mitigate them, which the first Makers of them had; every Law must also have some present known Person in Being, whose Will it must be to make it a Law for the Present; this cannot be said of the major Part of any Assembly, because that major part instantly ceaseth, as soon as ever it hath voted: an infallible Argument whereof is this, that the same major part after the Vote given, hath no Power to correct, alter, or mitigate it, or to Cause it to be put in Execution; so that he that shall act, or cause that Law to be executed, makes himself the Commander, or willer of it, which was originally the Will of others: It is said by Mr. *Hobs* in his *Leviathan,* page 141. *Nothing is Law, where the Legislator cannot be known, for there must be manifest Signs, that it proceedeth from the Will of the Soveraign; there is requisite, not only a Declaration of the Law, but also sufficient Signs of the Author and the Authority.*[37]

When the legislative power is in an assembly, therefore, the rapid succession of majorities amounts to a rapid succession of rulers, which is anarchy.[38] There is the further objection that there is lacking that continuous will which is necessary to sustain law. Popular government is therefore an impossibility.

The Supreme Power being an indivisible Beam of Majesty, cannot be divided among, or settled upon a Multitude. God would have it fixed in one Person, not sometimes in one part of the People, and sometimes in another; and sometimes, and that for the most part, no where, as when the Assembly is dissolved, it must rest in the Air, or in the walls of the Chamber where they were Assembled.[39]

---

[36] *Patriarcha,* p. 88.
[37] *Observations upon Aristotle's Politiques* (1696) p. 149.
[38] *Ibid.,* pp. 110-12.
[39] *Ibid.,* Preface.

Filmer adds makeweight arguments of little importance: he demonstrates that in Parliament most of the work is done by small committees, and necessarily so. Free discussion and deliberation by the entire body would make it impossible to get through the necessary business. But his main proof that government by an assembly is impossible is achieved by extorting the full meaning from the proposition that law is the will of the sovereign. No representative body can provide the continuous, undivided will necessary in a sovereign.

The Free-holders Grand Inquest Touching Our Sovereign Lord the King, and His Parliament[40] applies these general principles. Parliament derives its power from the writs of summons, which are the will of the king. The writs for election of members to the Commons provide only that they may petition, and consequently that is the extent of their power. The Lords are summoned to advise, but they have no legislative power; and their judicial power is exercised only by the king's favor. The king of England, like all kings, possesses complete and absolute authority. Oddly enough, Filmer speaks in the *Patriarcha* of the king's prerogative, a concept apparently useless in this setting. "The Court of *Chancery* itself is but a Branch of the King's Prerogative, to relieve men against the inexorable rigour of the Law, which without it is no better than a Tyrant, since *Summum Jus, is Summa Injuria.*"[41]

Less than any other thinker of his day, except Hobbes, Filmer insisted upon the moral character of government. His chief argument against the possibility of tyranny is that the interest of the king must necessarily coincide with that of his subjects.[42] But the patriarchal theory gives at least a flavor of purpose to the arbitrary will which Filmer places in his sovereign. Clearly he expected the

---

[40] This work is attributed to Filmer, but J. W. Allen says it is "certainly not his." "Sir Robert Filmer," *Social and Political Ideas of Some English Thinkers of the Augustan Age* (ed. Hearnshaw) p. 28. C. H. McIlwain says it is "probably the work of Sir Robert Holborne." *Political Works of James I*, p. c.

[41] p. 99.

[42] *Observations upon Aristotle's Politiques*, p. 109.

king to act for the benefit of his subjects, even though that was not the essential feature of his power. Peace and religion, he notes, have existed only in monarchies, not in the modified anarchy which passes for republican government.[43]

Filmer himself has provided us with a concise summary of his theory:[44] "1. *That there is no Form of Government, but Monarchy only. 2. That there is no Monarchy, but Paternal. 3. That there is no Paternal Monarchy, but Absolute, or Arbitrary. 4. That there is no such thing as an Aristocracy or Democracy. 5. That there is no such Form of Government as a Tyranny. 6. That the People are not born Free by Nature.*" The second step can be omitted without seriously impairing the argument.

The modern reader is likely to find Filmer's doctrine of sovereignty familiar enough, but is astounded by the assertion that sovereign power must necessarily be vested in one person, that monarchy is the only possible form of government. We have today non-monarchical governments which do in fact maintain peace and religion as efficiently as any monarchy. But if Filmer had difficulty in fitting his theory of sovereignty to governments, we have equal difficulty in fitting our governments to our theory of sovereignty. Only by some admitted fiction, such as Rousseau's general will or Willoughby's juristic person, can we reconcile the indivisible sovereign with popular government.

IV

Charles I never rose to the level of political theory. His reliance was upon the absolute, indisputable, and inseparable prerogative conferred upon him by the laws of England. He interpreted this to give him authority to take any action necessary for the welfare of the country. He told the Parliament of 1628: "if you (which God forbid) should not do your Duties in contributing what this State

---

[43] *Ibid.*, pp. 110-12.
[44] *Ibid.*, p. 151.

at this time needs, I must, in Discharge of my Conscience, use those other means which God hath put into my Hands, to save that the Follies of particular Men may otherwise hazard to lose." [45] And the Lord Keeper added, "Remember His Majesty's Admonition; I say, remember it." In like terms Charles protested to the Lords against the Petition of Right:[46]

We find it still insisted on, that in no case whatsoever, should it never so nearly concern matters of State and Government, we or our Privy Council have power to commit any one man without the cause be shewed. The service itself would be thereby destroyed and defeated, and the cause itself must be such as may be determined by our Judges of our Courts at *Westminster* in a legal and ordinary way of Justice; Whereas the cause may be such, as the Judges have not capacity of Judicature, nor rules of law to direct and guide their judgments in cases of transcendent nature, which happening so often, the very intermitting of the constant Rules of Government for so many ages within this Kingdom practiced, would soon dissolve the very frame and foundation of our monarchy: . . . so my Lords, we have thought good to let you know, that without the overthrow of our Sovereignty we cannot suffer this power to be impeached. . . .

The general theory upon which Charles relied was exactly that of Fleming, Bacon, Davies, and the earlier Coke. But to treat the failure of Parliament to vote subsidies as an emergency requiring extra-legal taxation was something entirely new. The problem was new, for on the one hand the king's needs were greater than ever before, and on the other hand Parliament was more obstinate than ever in demanding a *quid pro quo*.[47] In such a situation the old formulas would not work. But if "law of state" was inadequate as a solution to the problem, it should be pointed out that Charles' strictures on the supremacy of common law also were well grounded.

On one other subject Charles delivered himself of a very sugges-

---

[45] *Lords Journal*, iii, 687.

[46] *Bibliotheca Regia* (1659) p. 320.

[47] Peter Heylyn says: "The Commons, since the time of King James, have seldome parted with a peny, but they have paid themselves well for it out of the Prerogative." *A Short View of the Life and Reign of King Charles* (London, 1658) p. 32.

tive opinion. Unquestionably he considered the Church of England an institution as deeply rooted in national law as the monarchy itself. This raises the question debated during the Tractarian Movement in the nineteenth century, the problem of the relation of the Church to the political sovereign. This delicate issue was boldly faced by Hobbes, but most contemporary theorists shirked it. The contribution of Charles is so slight that it perhaps should not be given much weight; nevertheless, he did state that the Church was a corporation distinct from and independent of the political authority. When Parliament was negotiating with Charles at the conclusion of the First Civil War in an attempt to reach an acceptable settlement, Charles insisted obdurately upon the rights of the Anglican Church. He was bound by oath to the Church, he said, to preserve it. When Parliament offered to relieve him of that oath, he replied that this was beyond its power; the oath was not to Parliament, or to the kingdom, but to the Church.[48] Possibly this insistence upon the distinct existence of the Church foreshadows the pluralist arguments of Laski.

On another occasion, certainly, Charles did take a pluralist position, when he insisted in 1642 that England was a mixed monarchy of three distinct partners. But obviously this position was adopted for tactical advantage, and does not represent Charles' actual convictions. The absolute prerogative was his true philosophy of politics.

---

[48] Charles to Alexander Henderson, June 6, 1646: "Now, it must be known, to whom this Oath hath reference, and to *whose benefit?* the Answer is clear, onely to the *Church of England;* as by the Record will be plainly made appear; and you must mistake in alleaging, that the two *Houses of Parliament* (especially as they are now constituted) can have this *Disobligatory power,* for, (besides that they are not named in it) I am confident to made it clearly appear to you, that this *Church* never did submit, nor was subordinate to them; and that it was onely the *King* and *Clergy,* who made the *Reformation,* the *Parliament* meerly serving to help to give the *civil Sanction:* all this being proved (of which I make no question) it must necessarily follow, that it is onely the *Church of England* (in whose favour I took this Oath) that can release Me from it: wherefore when the Church of England (being lawfully assembled) shall declare that I am free, then, and not before, I shall esteem My self so." *Reliquiae Sacrae Carolinae* (The Hague, 1650) p. 199.

Chapter VII

THE CIVIL WAR PERIOD

I. *Parliament as the great council; Parliament as trustee for
the kingdom; the distinction between the office and the
person of the king; the emergency doctrine; mixed monarchy; the separation of powers; the contract theory.*

II. *Royalist arguments; interpretations.*

MUCH of the thought of the Civil War period has only
an indirect relation to the constitutional controversies
of the period 1603-40. Especially on the anti-royalist
side novel arguments were introduced. The whole contract theory
was in England a thing without antecedents, except for its literary
use by such men as Hooker. Moreover, the huge volume of the
literature, as well as the great variety of the arguments, makes it
impractical to subjoin any general discussion of Civil War theory
to a study the main concern of which is with the earlier period.
But it is possible to trace through the years 1640-49 a development
of some of the lines of argument treated in earlier chapters. A
sketch of these topics may form a conclusion to the foregoing discussion; it will form hardly an introduction to the whole subject of
Civil War theory.

I

The pattern of the thought of the Long Parliament is dimly
traceable in the stubborn insistence of the Parliament of 1621 that it
had the right to advise the king in foreign affairs, and in the repeated efforts of later Parliaments to determine national policies.
Parliament was the king's great council—so Pym argued in the

'20's as in the '40's; it was empowered to advise him *de quibusdam arduis et urgentibus negotiis,* as the writ of summons recited.

According to the Long Parliament this was a duty as well as a right. The Parliament was the representative body of the kingdom and was charged with a trust on its behalf,[1] a claim which drew from Charles the reply that "he had often heard of the great trust, that by the law of God and man, was committed to the king for the defence and safety of his people; but as yet he never understood what trust or power was committed to either or both houses of parliament without the king; they being summoned to council and advise the king." [2] This was a position which Parliament assumed without debating it. Yet it is a claim of enormous import. Not the law, but the kingdom, is now the object of concern; and Parliamentary sovereignty lacks only avowal. The king also is a trustee, but his trusteeship brings duties without powers. The Long Parliament did not openly deny that he might legally refuse to perform his duties, but it was obliged to arrive at some such result in order to perfect its own trusteeship. Parliamentary argument passed through three stages: the claim of exclusive right to counsel the king; the adoption of the doctrine of the Despencers; and the adoption of the emergency doctrine.

The privy councillors whom the Long Parliament forced upon Charles in 1640 refused to counsel him; he was to be guided, they said, only by his great council, the Parliament.[3] The Earl of Essex told Hyde, "that the king was obliged in conscience to conform himself, and his own understanding, to the advice and conscience of his Parliament." [4] It followed that persons who presumed to advise the king were "evil councillors"; they were speedily erected into the "malignant party" which in Parliamentary theory held Charles (or the better nature of Charles) prisoner, and from which

---

[1] Clarendon, *History of the Rebellion,* V, 107.
[2] *Ibid.,* V, 112.
[3] *Ibid.,* III, 54, 197.
[4] *Ibid.,* III, 165.

Parliament loyally and respectfully endeavored to rescue him. Thus the modest Parliamentary appeal of the '20's, "from Caesar ill-informed to Caesar well-informed," was converted to an appeal from Caesar privately advised to Caesar advised by his Parliament.

So a man who advised the king contrary to the advice of Parliament was voted "an enemy to the king and kingdom," and a committee was appointed to discover the malefactor.[5] Thereafter, in large part, the Parliament relied upon this device of evil councillors, taking great credit for imputing no malice to the king: "how often and undutifully soever those wicked counsellors should fix their dishonour upon the king, by making his majesty the author of those evil actions which were the effects of their own evil counsels, they, his majesty's loyal and dutiful subjects, could use no other style, according to that maxim of the law, *the king can do no wrong;* but if any ill were committed in matter of state, the council, if in matter of justice, the judges must answer for it."[6] This line of thought culminated in the demand made in the Nineteen Propositions that the king employ as privy councillors only persons approved by Parliament.[7]

But this did not solve the main problem; it did not enable the Parliament to legislate without the king. The only legal solution of the difficulty was the adoption of the treasonable doctrine of the Despencers, the argument that legal rights belonged to the office of the king, and when the king in his person refused justice

---

[5] *Ibid.,* IV, 285.

[6] *Ibid.,* V, 165. This argument made its appearance as early as 1640, when Glanvill, Speaker of the Short Parliament, told Charles: "The King can do no wrong; if, therefore, by the Subtilty of Mis-informers, by the specious and false Pretences of Public Good, by cunning and close Contrivance of their Ways to seduce, the Sacred Person shall, at any time, be circumvented, or surprized, or over-wrought, and drawn to command Things contrary to Law; and that the same be done accordingly; these Commands will be void, and the king innocent, even in his very Person, defended by his Prerogative; nevertheless the Authors of such Mis-informations, and Actors in those Abuses, will stand liable and exposed to strict Examination and just Censure, as having nothing to defend themselves but the Colour of a void Command, made void by just Prerogative, and by the fundamental and true Reason of State and Monarchy; and what Difference is there, or can be, in Law, between a void Command and no Command at all?" *Lords Journal,* iv, 51.

[7] Clarendon, *op. cit.,* V, 321.

the duties of the office should be discharged by Parliament. This distinction between the office and the man had been the basis of an attainder, and had been expressly denounced in Calvin's Case;[8] Parliament sidled into this position with discomfort and uncertainty, and never frankly avowed its stand. It defended Hotham's seizure of the arsenal at Hull, insisting that the public property of the kingdom did not belong to the king, but to the kingdom, for whom it was held in trust: "the very jewels of the Crown are not the King's proper goods, but are only intrusted to him for the use and Ornament thereof."[9] It asserted that kings are in conscience obliged to assent to bills offered them by Parliament in the name and for the good of the whole kingdom; Parliament is the fittest judge of whether or not a bill is for the common good. The Parliament is "a Councell to provide for the necessity, to prevent the imminent dangers, and preserve the publike peace and safety of the Kingdom, and to declare the Kings pleasure in those things as are requisite thereunto, and what they do herein hath the stampe of Royall authority, although his Majesty seduced by evill Councell, do in his own person oppose or interrupt the same for the Kings Supream power and Royall pleasure is exercised and declared in this high court of Law and Councell after a more eminent and obligatory manner, then it can be by any personall Act or Resolution of his own. . . . And the high Court of Parliament and all other his Majesties Officers and ministers ought to be subservient to that power and authority which Law hath placed in his Majesty to that purpose, though he himselfe in his owne person should neglect the same."[10]

To this the king replied by citing Calvin's Case, and the Parliament retorted with an even more elaborate distinction between the

---

[8] See *supra*, p. 51.

[9] *An Exact Collection of all Remonstrances, etc. between the Kings Most Excellent Majesty and his High Court of Parliament, December, 1641–March 21, 1643* (London, 1642-3) p. 266.

[10] *Ibid.*, p. 302 ff.

person and the office of the king. The argument entered a further stage:

There must be a Judge of that Question wherein the safety of the Kingdom depends (for it must not lie undetermined). If then there be not an agreement between his Majestie and his Parliament, either his Majestie must be the Judge against his Parliament, or the Parliament without his Majestie; If his Majestie against his Parliament, why not as well of the necessity in the Question of making a law without and against their consent, as of denying a Law against their desire and advice? The Judge of the necessity in either case by like reason is Judge in both; Besides, if his Majestie in this difference of opinions should be Judge, he should be judge in his own Case, but the Parliament should be Judges between his Majestie and the Kingdom, as they are in many, if not in all cases. And if his Majesty should be Judge he should be Judge out of his Courts and against his highest Court, which he never is, but the Parliament should onely judge without his Majesties personal consent, which as a Court of Judicature, it always doth, and all other Courts as well as it, if the King be for the Kingdom, and not the Kingdom for the King. And if the Kingdom best knows what is for its own good and preservation; and the Parliament be the Representative Body of the Kingdom, it is easy to judge who in this case should be the Judge. . . . We do not say this, as if the Royall Assent were not requisite in the passing of Laws nor do, or ever did we say, that because his Majesty is bound to give his consent to good Laws, presented to him in Parliament: that, therefore they shall be Laws without his consent or at all Obligatory. Saving only for the necessary preservation of the Kingdom whilst that necessity lasteth, and such consent cannot be obtained. [11]

This insistence that "his Majesties Authority is more in his Courts without his person, then in his person without his Courts" barely falls short of an absolute claim of power to govern without the king. What was lacking was pieced out by the doctrine of emergency. In cases of "extreme danger" the two houses might by ordinance legislate without the king, and the ordinance of the militia was only the first exercise of legislative power under pretense of necessity.[12]

These various positions were caught up and pressed to their ultimate conclusions by the pamphleteers of the Parliamen-

---

[11] *Ibid.*, p. 697.
[12] Clarendon, *op. cit.*, IV, 350.

tary party. Many zealous propagandists argued that the king in law possessed no "negative voice"; his veto power was usurped. The emergency doctrine should have caused some uneasiness to the veterans of the early Parliaments of Charles, who had denounced it as arbitrary rule, but Henry Parker turned the old royalist arguments against the king.[13]

Have the two houses a strict right to lay upon the people what taxes they judge meet? Have they power to pardon all Treasons, etc., sub intelligitur without the King's consent? We answer that they have not any such ordinary power, but if the Kingdom's safety lie upon it, and the King will not concur in saving the Kingdom in an ordinary way they may have recourse to extraordinary means for the saving of it: ordinarily the people may not take up arms but in the case of extraordinary invasion by foreign or domestic force they may justify the taking up of arms, and when war itself is justifiable all the necessary concomitants and expedients of a politic war are justifiable. Nature has confined water to a descending course yet not by such a rigid law but that for the necessary subvention of the whole fabric, and for the avoiding of that vacuity which nature more abhors than the dispensation or temporary suspension of such or such a particular inferior law, this ponderous element may forsake its ordinary course and mount upwards. In a village when houses stand scattered and remote 'tis not lawful for me to demolish this House because that which stands next is all of aflame, but in a city this is lawful where the Houses are so conjoined that the flame of one house may extend itself to the consuming or endangering of a whole street or more.

This is bad enough, but he continues:

Good Mr. Jenkins' policy is not to be superseded by law, but law is to be improved by policy, and as in quiet times and private cases 'tis safer to follow Law than Policy, so in times of troubles, and in affairs of general and great concernment 'tis safer to observe Policy than Law. The same may

---

[13] *Rejoinder of H. P. of Lincoln's Inn to Mr. David Jenkin's Cordial*, in *Judge Jenkins* (ed. W. H. Terry) p. 116. As Parker inherited the royalist position, the democrats inherited the old Parliamentary position, and Parker addressed to "free-born" John Lilburne the same rebuke that had been administered to Eliot: "if you were not so unskill'd in the theory, as you are in the practise of the Law, you would not upon all occasions so often insist upon inconveniencies likely to ensue to your self, and take no notice of publick mischiefs. You would then be satisfied, that your Judges ought rather to admit of a mischief to you, then of an inconvenience to the State: although you perpetually urge them to admit of mischief to the state, rather then inconveniences to you." *A Letter of Dire Censure and Redargution to Lieut. Coll. John Lilburne* (London, 1650) p. 15. (This tract, however, has been attributed to Hugh Peters.)

be said of not pardoning, for doubtless the King has as much latitude to refuse, as to grant pardons, yet, when his power in either may be mischievous, his power in both must submit to reason of State, and law is not violated, but better improved, when true reason of State takes place above it.

Strafford was sent to the block for holding precisely these opinions. Here is all that was hateful to Coke and Eliot and their fellows. John Selden himself, who sat in the Long Parliament, at some time in his later years delivered himself of a biting criticism of this type of argument.[14]

There is not any thing in the World more abus'd then this Sentence *Salus populi suprema lex esto,* for wee apply it, as if wee ought to forsake the knowne law when it may bee most for the advantage of the people, when it meanes no such thing: for first, 'tis not *salus populi suprema lex est,* but *Esto,* it being one of the lawes of the 12 tables, & after divers lawes made, some for punishment, some for reward, then followes this, *salus populi suprema lex esto,* that in all the Lawes you make, have a speciall Eye to the good of the people: And then what does this concerne the way they now goe?

In the interchange of messages regarding Hull the king chiefly relied upon his obvious legal rights, but he also introduced what is perhaps the first clear-cut description of England as a mixed monarchy in literature, if one excepts the doubtful expressions of Fortescue.[15] In the earlier Stuart Parliaments England was a "legal"

---

[14] *Table-Talk* (ed. Pollock) p. 93.

[15] *An Exact Collection, etc.,* p. 320 ff.
Apparently Fortescue's *dominium politicum et regale* was monarchy limited by law rather than "mixed" monarchy; see Professor McIlwain's argument, *Growth of Political Thought in the West,* p. 357 ff. Camden approves Fortescue, saying: "Regall authority is where the king without assent or knowledge of his people may make laws that are not grievous. . . . Political authority is where the King can make no lawes without the assent and consent of his people." "A Discourse concerning the Prerogative of the Crown," in the hand of Camden, Stowe Mss., 237. There was little or no precise thinking on this subject before the Civil War, as Raleigh's classification shows: "Monarchies are of 2 sorts touching their power or authority; *viz.* 1. Intire, where the whole power of ordering all state matters, both in peace and warre, doth by law and custom appertain to the prince, as in the English kingdome, where the prince hath power to make lawes, league and warre, to create magistrates, to pardon life, of appeale, & c. Though, to give a contentment to the other degrees, they have a suffrage in making lawes; yet ever subject to the princes pleasure, or negative will. 2. Limited, or restrained, that hath no full power . . . as the Polonian kings." *The Prince, or Maximes of State, Somers Tracts,* iii, 283. Probably it is safe to say that Hooker represents the English tradition; there is no question but that his monarchy is merely limited, not mixed. But after 1642 monarchy is mixed, as with

monarchy; the king was considered to be limited by law.[16] Now for the first time the constitution becomes a social rather than a legal institution; it is Aristotle's familiar balance of classes.[17] The royal power is not limited, but shared; the state is not legal, but pluralistic.

There being three kindes of Government amongst men, Absolute Monarchy, Aristocracy, and Democracy, and all these having their particular conveniences and inconveniences. The experience and wisdom of your Ancestors hath so moulded this out of a mixture of these, as to give to this Kingdome (as far as human Prudence can provide) the conveniences of all three, without the inconveniences of any one, as long as the Balance hangs even between the three Estates, and they run joyntly on in their proper Chanell (begetting Verdure and Fertility in the Meadows on both sides) and the overflowing of either on either side raise no deluge or Inundation. The ill of absolute monarchy is tyranny, the ill of Aristocracy is Faction and Division, the ills of Democracy are Tumults, Violence, and Licentiousnesse. The good of Monarchy is the uniting of a Nation under one Head to resist Invasion from abroad, and Insurrection at home: the good of Aristocracy is the Conjunction of Counsell in the ablest Persons of a State for the publick benefit: the good of Democracy is Liberty, and the Courage and Industry which Liberty begets.

In this Kingdome the Laws are joyntly made by a King, by a House of Peers, and by a House of Commons chosen by the People, all having free Votes and particular Priviledges: the Government according to these Laws is trusted to the King, Power of Treaties, of War and Peace, of making Peers, of choosing Officers and Councellours for State, Judges for Law, Commanders of Forts and Castles, giving Commissions for raising men to make Warre abroad, or to prevent or provide against Invasions or Insurrections at home, benefit of Confiscations, power of pardoning, and some of the like kinde are placed in the King. And this kind of regulated Monarchy having this power to preserve that Authority, without which it would be disabled to preserve the Laws in their Force, and the Subjects in their liberties and proprieties, is intended to draw to him such a Respect and Relation from

---

Sir Roger Twysden, who says: "Cavaliero Francis Biondy, an Italian writer of great worth and honour, in his Introduction to the Civil Wars of York and Lancaster, speaks very judiciously of the foundations upon which this kingdome is built, and the happy estate the people are in who live under such a mixture, as hee termes, 'una ben constituita aristodemocratica monarchia.' " *Certaine Considerations upon the Government of England* (Camden Society) p. 14.

[16] *Parliamentary Debates in 1610* (Camden Society, ed. Gardiner) p. 89.

[17] Discussions of mixed monarchy are common in 1642; of course it is not possible to say positively that none antedates this reply to the Nineteen Propositions, in June, 1642.

the great Ones, as may hinder the ills of Division and Faction and such a Feare and Reverence from the people, as may hinder Tumults, Violence, and licenciousnesse. Again, that the Prince may not make use of this high and perpetuall power to the hurt of those for whose good he hath it, and make use of the name of Publick Necessitie for the gain of his private Favorites and Followers, to the detriment of his People, the House of Commons (an excellent Conserver of Liberty, but never intended for any share in Government, or the chusing of them that should govern) is solely intrusted with the first propositions concerning the Leavies of Moneys (which is the sinewes as well of Peace as War) and the impeaching of those, who for their owne ends, though countenanced by any surreptitiously gotten Command of the King have violated that Law, which he is bound (when he knows it) to protect, and to the protection of which they are bound to advise him, at least not to serve him in the contrary. And the Lords being trusted with a Judicatorie power, are an excellent Screen and Bank between the Prince and the People, to assist each against any Incroachments of the other, and by just Judgments to preserve that Law, which ought to be the Rule of every one of the three.

Here is the theory of the balanced constitution, with legislative power in the three estates, power of government in the king, and power of judicature in the Lords, which Montesquieu a hundred years later thought the most admirable device in the world. It was for Charles an admirable device: it rationalized English law in terms of political theory, and gave to him what Calhoun's pluralistic system gave to the southern states, the concurrent veto.[18] It was taken up at once by such royalist writers as Dr. Henry Ferne, and by Parliamentary writers like Henry Parker, and became the commonplace of constitutional discussion that it remained until Bagehot. The Parliamentarians, however, were not able to explain away the King's veto. Philip Hunton argued in his *Treatise of Monarchy* that in a mixed monarchy the nobility and commons should restrain the king if he "run in any course tending to the dissolving of the constituted frame"; this is the very purpose of mixed monarchies, "that one should counterpoize and keep even

---

[18] On the pluralism of Calhoun see Wiltse, "Calhoun and the Modern State," *Virginia Quarterly Review*, xiii, 396.

the other." [19] But what becomes of the compact on which Hunton so firmly grounds his commonwealth, if two parties to the compact may invade the rights of the third?

A very neat solution, achieved it is true by doing great violence to English law, was set forth by John Sadler in 1649.[20] Led on by a mystical reverence for the number three, he completed the anticipation of Montesquieu by expounding the theory of the separation of powers; he attached each of the powers to a distinct estate.

It may be considered, that many Kingdoms, and Commonwealths (that were not Kingdoms) in all Ages did consist of *Three Estates;* (as of *Three Principles* in Nature, or Bodies Naturall;) which might occasion the Phrase of *Tribe,* in many other besides the *Romans;* who in *Three Estates,* were not so Ancient as the *Grecians* or *Egyptians;* that I speak not of the *Gauls, Britons,* or the *Eastern* Nations.

And if any would observe, it might be possible to find the Prophets hinting a Trinity in divers Kingdoms or Estates; and that not only for moulding, but for overthrowing them: Besides the Three Captivities, or Three overturnings of the Jewish State; and the Three blows of the Goat on the *Ram* in Daniel; as alluding to the Three great Battles which did break the *Persian* Empire.

And why may not the sacred Trinity be shadowed out in Bodies *Politick,* as well as in *Natural?* And if so, our Three Estates may be branched as our *Writs,* into *Original, Judicial,* and *Executive;* as shadows of the *Being, Wisdom,* and *Activity* Divine.

If I may not grant, yet I cannot deny *Original* Power to the Commons; *Judicial* to the Lords, *Executive* to the King; as the Spirit to the Body, or if you will, the *Head* (or Fountain of Sense and Motion;) But he must *see* by two *Eyes,* and hear by two *Ears;* as I touched before, yet his very *pardoning* although it be by Law much limited, doth seeme to speak his Power *Executive:* And so his *Writs* do speak aright; *Because my Courts have so, and so judged: Therefore I do so, and so command the Judgment shall be executed.* And if any will assert the *Militia,* to this Power Executive, I shall also grant it to the *King;* so that it may always be under the Power *Original* and *Judicial.*

This might belong to the *Lords,* and that to the *Commons,* and the plain

---

[19] Part I, Chap. IV.

[20] *Rights of the Kingdome: or, Customs of our Ancestors, Touching the Duty, Power, Election, or Succession of our Kings and Parliaments, Our True Liberty, due Allegiance, three Estates, their Legislative Power, Original, Judicial, and Executive, with the Militia.* The quotations are from the edition of 1682.

truth is, I do not find more Arguments to prove the *Judicial* Power to belong to the *Lords,* than I do for the *Legislative* in the *Commons:* And (as it seemeth to be above, so *below* also) it may be much disputed, That the *Legislative, Judicial,* and *Executive* power, should be in distinct Subjects by the Law of *Nature.*

For If *Law-makers* be *Judges* of those that break their Laws, they seem to Judge in their own Causes: which our Law, and Nature itself so much avoideth and abhorreth. So it seemeth also to forbid both the *Lawmaker* and *Judge* to *execute:* And by express Act of Parliament, it is provided, that Sheriffs be not *Justices,* where they be *Sheriffs.* But if *Execution* be always consonant to *Judgment,* and this to *Law;* there is still most sweet Harmony, and as I may say, a *Sacred Unity* in *Trinity* represented.

That the Commons should have most Right to the Power *Original,* or *Legislative* in *Nature;* I shall leave to be disputed by others.

There follows an interesting argument that only the ancient barons by tenure possessed a native judicial power, and peers by patent or writ were merely the king's commissioned judges. And he concludes: "and besides all that was said before, this seemeth one Reason, why our Ancestors did so willingly follow the Vice [Voice] of *Nature,* in placing the Power *Legislative, Judicial* and *Executive,* in three distinct Estates (as in Animals, Aerials, Etherials or Celestials, three regions, and three principles in *Naturals,*) that so they might be forced to consult often and much in all they did."

Of course the main contribution of Civil War theory is the development of the contract theory of government. But this was the work of pamphleteers. As again in 1689, Parliament during the Civil War chose to rely upon legal arguments rather than political theories. Pym, it is true, in his argument against Strafford, spoke of "the Pact and Covenant betwixt the King and his people." [21] Other individual Parliamentarians professed allegiance to the contract theory. And when the king began to raise a troop at York the two houses voted: "That whensoever the king maketh war upon the parliament, it is a breach of the trust reposed in him by his

---

[21] *Speeches and Passages of this Great and Happy Parliament* (London, 1641).

people; contrary to his oath; and tending to the dissolution of the government."[22] Implicit in this is the theory of contract. But the theory was not made explicit; even in 1649 it was for alleged violation of law that Charles Stuart was brought to trial.

II

Royalist argument underwent no striking development during the Civil War. No extravagant claims were necessary. Parliament, not the court, was guilty of innovation and usurpation; Charles was the champion of the fundamental laws and the rights of the subjects. So the men whose gospel was the common law of Coke rallied to him, and Judge Jenkins, for example, poured from the Tower denunciations of the Parliament and demonstrations of the legal rights of the king. Charles himself took the legalistic position when, upon the advice of Hale, he refused to acknowledge the jurisdiction of the High Court of Justice that tried him, as a body unknown to the laws of England.

Other familiar arguments were employed. Many clerical supporters of Charles, with wearisome citation of Scripture, enjoined passive obedience. The various elements of earlier royalist thought appeared in fragments in numerous badly argued tracts. The variety and the disorderliness of the arguments are illustrated by a *Panegyrick upon Monarchy*[23] published in 1658.

> It is the image of that Domination,
> By which Jehovah rules the whole Creation. . . .
> As old as that paternal Sovereignty
> God placed in Adam, rul'd his People by. . . .
> The Antients did a Monarchy prefer,
> Made all their Gods submit to *Jupiter;*
> And (when affairs and Nations first began)
> Princes' Decrees were th' only Laws of Man;
>   Experience will avow it, where there's any,
>   *One Honest Man* is sooner found than Many.

---

[22] Clarendon, *op. cit.,* V, 142.
[23] *Roxburghe Ballads* (1884-5), Vol. 5, p. 8. The text is from a version of 1685.

The Rational Soul performs a Prince's part,
She rules the Body by Monarchick Art;
Poor Cranes, and silly Bees (with shivering Wings,)
Observe their Leaders, and obey their Kings:
   Nature herself disdains a crowded throne,
   The Body's Monstrous, has more Heads than One.

A monarchy's that Politick simple State,
Consists in Unity (inseparate,
Pure and entire); a Government that stands
When others fall, touch'd but with levelling hands;
   So Natural, and with such Skill endu'd,
   It makes One Body of a Multitude.

In Order (wherein latter things depend
On former) that's most perfect doth attend
On Unity; But this can never be
The Popular State, nor Aristocracy;
   For where or *All,* or *Many* bear the Sway,
   Such Order to Confusion leads the way.

So the old arguments were presented with less than the old skill. Perhaps the only significant contribution to political theory from the royalist side was the revival of the notion of mixed monarchy.[24] This was the philosophy of deadlock, which was indeed the highest demand of Charles in the Civil War. Since he could not make good his right to supremacy, he could at least claim to be an equal partner with the lords and commons. His claim to partnership was disallowed by the Long Parliament, but the idea endured, and mixed monarchy became the official theory of the Restoration.

When the crown stepped down from the position of sovereignty to the level of the other two estates, more was lost than the ancestral rights of the Stuarts. Not merely royalty, but government, was the loser. The work of the Tudors was stayed for a hundred and fifty years. The old Alsatias of property and feudal privilege against which Henry VII had directed the power of the crown made good

---

[24] See *supra*, p. 114.

their claim to immunity from governmental control, and the fate of Strafford, a champion not of despotism but of administration, foreshadowed the failure of Turgot. This is not to suggest that the Stuarts were levellers, or that the opposition to the Stuarts was conspicuously propertied or feudal. This collision was merely incidental to a larger conflict; but it is a fact that the interests of government were on the one side, and the interests of privilege on the other. In so small a matter as the personnel of the civil service this is to be seen. Laud was denounced by the Parliamentarians as the son of a butcher; it was nearly three hundred years before a man so meanly born again stood at the king's right hand. The civil service of Charles was a weak instrument, but it was integrity itself beside that of Walpole.

Among other things, the issue was between what the French distinguish as administration and justice. In France, where the principles of Turgot worked themselves out under Napoleon, the superiority of administration and administrative courts to private concerns and the ordinary courts was eventually established. It was at this that Berkeley aimed when he said, "There is a rule of law and a rule of government, and many things may be done by the rule of government that may not be done by the rule of law." The Long Parliament charged these words against Berkeley as high treason,[25] and the fact that the Long Parliament itself was obliged to rely upon the principle did not prevent its eventual repudiation.

Certainly there is much that is immediately wholesome in the English regard for private right and fixed rules of law. But the background of that attitude is not wholesome. The background is the feudal ideal of a static law and a static social system, in which government performs merely the police function and the adjudication of *meum* and *tuum*. And this was the background of the

---

[25] *Articles of Accusation against the Judges* (London, 1641). See *The Journal of Sir Simonds D'Ewes* (ed. Notestein) p. 354n. for the debate.

Restoration settlement. The mixed monarchy no less than the earlier Parliamentary position implies a scheme of natural law. It is society expressed in terms of social elements, rather than in terms immediately of law; but it negates sovereignty, and by adopting the philosophy of deadlock affirms a belief in a fixed order of things. Like any pluralist society, it proclaims the right to autonomy of its elements, the right to the concurrent veto. It proclaims the stability and justice of a society so ordered, a faith which history has not justified.

What the Stuarts stood for was the principle of the monistic state, the doctrine of Hobbes and Rousseau and Maistre. The royalist insistence upon the organizing rôle of command resulted from a conviction of the necessity of government and of sovereignty, a doubt as to the existence of a unifying natural law, a belief in the fundamental instability of society. Perhaps, as has often been suggested, the immediate occasion for the royalist claim of sovereignty was the rivalry of international Catholicism; but this rivalry is merely an illustration of the disruptive forces in society which demand monistic control. Perhaps when Filmer insisted that no state could endure without an absolute monarch he was arguing that no society will naturally cohere, that without guidance it will split into many petty principalities—that affirmative action is necessary, and that this action must be coordinated and directed. Perhaps he was right.

INDEX